79-973

WITHDRAWN

INVOLUNTARY TREATMENT
OF THE MENTALLY ILL

Publication Number 979

AMERICAN LECTURE SERIES

A Monograph in
The BANNERSTONE DIVISION *of*
AMERICAN LECTURES IN BEHAVIORAL SCIENCE AND LAW

Edited by
RALPH SLOVENKO, B.E., L.L.B., M.A., Ph.D.
Wayne State University
Law School
Detroit, Michigan

INVOLUNTARY TREATMENT OF THE MENTALLY ILL

The Problem of Autonomy

By

MICHAEL ALFRED PESZKE, M.D.

Associate Professor
University of Connecticut School of Medicine
(Farmington, Connecticut)
Diplomate
American Boards of Psychiatry

CHARLES C THOMAS • **PUBLISHER**
Springfield • Illinois • U. S. A.

Published and Distributed Throughout the World by
CHARLES C THOMAS • PUBLISHER
Bannerstone House
301-327 East Lawrence Avenue, Springfield, Illinois, U.S.A.

© *1975, by* CHARLES C THOMAS • PUBLISHER
ISBN 0-398-03373-0
Library of Congress Catalog Card Number: 74-26682

With THOMAS BOOKS *careful attention is given to all details of
manufacturing and design. It is the Publisher's desire to present books that are
satisfactory as to their physical qualities and artistic possibilities and
appropriate for their particular use.* THOMAS BOOKS *will be true to those
laws of quality that assure a good name and good will.*

Printed in the United States of America
R-1

Library of Congress Cataloging in Publication Data
Peszke, Michael Alfred.
    Involuntary treatment of the mentally ill.

    (American lecture series ; publication no. 979 : A
monograph in the Bannerstone division of American
lectures
in behavioral science and law)
    Bibliography: p.
    Includes index.
    1. Insanity—Jurisprudence—United States. 2. Mental
health laws—United States. I. Title.
    [DNLM: 1. Forensic
Psychiatry. 2. Hospitalization. 3. Mental
disordersTherapy. W740 p476i]
KF480.p48   344'.73'044   74-26682
ISBN 0-398-03373-0

To my Parents,
with gratitude

INTRODUCTION

This monograph deals with the problem of involuntary commitment of the mentally ill to psychiatric institutions for involuntary treatment.

It is a topic which is of growing concern to many attorneys, and to an increasing number of sociologists and political scientists. It is a topic which should be of significant concern to *every* physician and, indeed, to *every* citizen, since it may affect his potential right to treatment or possibly lead to abridgment of some of his liberties.

The problem can be viewed as a conflict over the perception of and the commitment to autonomy. Webster defines autonomy as, "The quality or state of being independent, free and self-directing," and "Possession of moral freedom of self-determination."

It is this issue that the monograph confronts; it presents the legal repugnance at inflicting treatment involuntarily and the medical wish to ensure that very autonomy which is impeded and constricted by the coercion of mental illness.

The monograph is written primarily from a medical point of view. It is written for the lay person who is interested in this problem and who, perhaps, has been exposed to a veritable barrage of polemics dealing with this question. It is written for the medical student and the physician, to acquaint them with some of the legal concerns about this traditionally medical practice. It is written for the attorney to give him a better historical and medical perspective of a problem which has its roots in antiquity and for which there have been no constructive alternatives. It is not a compendium of advice on how, when and whom to commit; nor is it a guide for the physician on how to avoid being sued. It is not a comprehensive review of the different statutes and practices in the fifty states of the union, and for that

vii

the reader is referred to the excellent study by Brakel and Rock. (1)

The topic has, in the last few years, become one of the major sources of concern and acrimony both within psychiatric ranks as well as between psychiatry and the legal profession. It is not merely an academic issue, but one which affects thousands of individuals who are either neglected medically to protect their civil rights, or who are often committed for treatment in ways which are degrading and unreasonable, if not unnecessary, to institutions that provide little more than custodial care.

In the body of the monograph I use "psychiatry" and "medicine" and "physician" and "psychiatrist" interchangeably. I do this for a definite reason, and not merely because of carelessness. Psychiatry is not a profession; it is a specialty of the profession of medicine. This fact is very poorly understood. Psychiatrists are not licensed to practice psychiatry any more than surgeons are licensed to practice surgery or ophthalmologists to practice ophthalmology. This may happen in the future, but currently in all states of the union there is only one basic medical license granted to all physicians, whether it be the practice of general medicine or of specialty medicine. Psychiatrists, like other specialists, have specialty boards which are voluntarily taken and on the passing of which the specialist is referred to as "Board Qualified" in the area of his expertise.

There is one other reason why I use the terms "physician" and "psychiatrist" interchangeably. Most jurisdictions in the United States, as well as in Europe, do not limit the statutory powers for emergency detention or commitment to psychiatric institutions *solely* to psychiatrists. In all of the jurisdictions, every physician is entitled to the same powers of emergency commitment as he is entitled and trained to perform an emergency tracheostomy. Undoubtedly, many physicians go through their professional lives without ever having become involved with an acute psychiatric problem, but some, particularly in general practice or those who staff emergency rooms, are confronted with such problems frequently, and all jurisdictions allow them to exercise this option. The model here is medical. All physicians are, in theory at least, taught to diagnose every kind of problem and then to refer for further consultation and treatment to an appropriate specialist when necessary. The process of commitment follows this model, in that the physician confronted with an acute psychiatric emergency makes a disposition to a psychiatric hospital where psychiatrists begin their own diagnostic and therapeutic interventions. Most statutes also specify that the admitting physician, if he or she feels that the commitment was unnecessary, is allowed to refuse such a commitment.

I am convinced that the two professions polarized over this issue, namely Law and Medicine, have at least one common denominator of agreement — namely, concern about the citizen's basic rights, including his right to autonomy.

It is my hope that this concern will preclude ascerbic insults and lead to thoughtful studies and mutual cooperation to ensure that the most enlightened and acceptable level of care is given to the ill, that no citizen is ever deprived of any right, whether it be to health or to freedom, and that nothing is allowed to infringe upon the autonomy of the citizens of not only the United States, but of the world.

NOTE

1. S. J. Brakel, and R. S. Rock, *The Mentally Disabled and the Law* (Chicago, University of Chicago Press, 1971).

ACKNOWLEDGMENTS

I WISH particularly to acknowledge Professor Ralph Slovenko's encouragement. His support and that of Mr. Payne Thomas and Mr. W. N. Lyon of Charles C Thomas, Publisher were instrumental in my embarking on this effort.

I have to express deep appreciation to the University of Connecticut Research Foundation, Dr. Hugh Clark, Chairman, for assistance in obtaining secretarial help and to the head of the Department of Psychiatry, Professor Benjamin Wiesel, for arranging my schedule in such a way that I had both the time and the opportunity to do the necessary research. Professor Wiesel's obstacle-breaking optimism and the constant equanimity of the department's administrative director, Mrs. Karen Lynch, were constant encouragements whenever I confronted difficulties.

The reference librarian of the University of Connecticut Health Center, Mrs. Robbie Kolman, and her staff most graciously answered all my requests for historical and other idiosyncratic reference material, obtained it as a moment's notice, and assisted me in the most indefatigable manner.

Last, but not least, I want to thank my secretary, Mrs. Helen Wheeler, for having typed out numerous versions of the manuscript with patience and good humor, and Ms. Nancy Crothers who was helpful in the final editing and typing of the manuscript.

My long-suffering and patient family have also to be thanked, since occasionally during their impatient moments they showed how easily this whole work could have been sabotaged by them.

M.A.P.

CONTENTS

INVOLUNTARY TREATMENT
OF THE MENTALLY ILL

CHAPTER I

HISTORICAL AND PHILOSOPHICAL PERSPECTIVES

THE history of psychiatry leaves one somewhat perplexed as to the actual entity of those psychological problems which, in historical times, fell within the scope of lunacy or insanity. We certainly read about states of the mind that are called "lunacy," "madness," or, at times, referred to specifically as "hysterias" or "melancholias." Such psychological deviations from accepted "normal" have been recognized by different cultures and at different historical times. Yet we cannot transpose Greek or medieval diagnostic labels to our own 20th century experience and knowledge or assume that to Burton melancholia was the same entity as unipolar depression. (1)

It is, furthermore, not clear how some of these entities would be conceived of in our day and age. This problem can be better appreciated when we consider that in our own 20th century with the ready way in which communications are exchanged, the ease with which people travel, knowledge and experience are not easily shared, and there is lack of agreement or concensus in current day psychiatry as to the primary etiology of most of our psychiatric diagnostic entities. There is even no reasonable cross-cultural acceptance of what is meant by "normal." (2) Cultural attitudes affect the symptomatology not only of such a phenomenon as the hysterical syndrome, but even seem to affect the behavior and primary symptomatology of schizophrenia. (3) Since we see such major differences due to culturally determined attributes in the forms of behavior between different national and ethnic groups and variations in diagnostic labelling between various medical centers in the United States, it becomes impossible to transpose the understanding of what was deviant behavior in Greek or medieval times to the present day. (4) If we take into account that our understanding of the world and of

3

science is markedly different, our thinking and perceptions consistently more abstract and less dogmatic than was the case in historically distant times, then it becomes even clearer that lunacy of those ancient days was not the same as our current label of psychosis.

We are aware from the various texts on the history of psychiatry that there was a constant polarity between explanations for maladaptive or peculiar behavior. Scientific on one hand (and that meant medical) and supernatural on the other (and this usually brought in the theologian or philosopher) were the two predominant etiological explanatory constructs. The scientific explanations attributing temperament and personality to different humors, or hysteria to the wandering uterus may amuse as naive and not very scholarly, but if contrasted with the supernatural theories, they have that quality, since they look for biological or social causation. (5) However, society of that time, (and even now with the popularity of exorcisms growing) readily explained all social crises, problems and illness as due to witchcraft and other nefarious influences. It is tempting to speculate whether the superior position with which we view the primative explanation of mental aberration and behavior is really justified now that the medical concept of mental illness is challenged by beliefs that the mentally ill are the victims of and caused by a devilish, perverse and hostile society. On the other hand, at the date of writing, not only has the etiological data for most forms of mental aberration not been documented, but there is growing awareness and conviction that a variety of factors are instrumental and important in the determination of the end product; namely, of the disease, so that whether we talk about a form of mental illness such as schizophrenia or of psychosomatic illness such as hypertension, we have to address ourselves both to inheritance (genetic factors) and to the environment (specifically to family surroundings). (6) Schizophrenia and hypertension (among others) are then end products of inherited factors, environmental influences, social and psychological, external and internal stresses, triggered by different frustrations and conflicts in the fulfillment of motivational drives and self-image.

They are, furthermore, compounded by economic and social

factors. This is one of the most difficult things to grasp either for the medical student or for the law student. Many of the college graduates who go on to professional schools have taken introductory courses in science or in sociology where the methodological research issues tend to give either "yes" or "no" answers. (7) These appear to be both scientifically valid and to give the illusion of definitive answers as to the issue involved. Thus, for example, such a complex question as, "Is mental hospital admission beneficial or detrimental?" cannot possibly be conceived of in "yes" or "no" terms, yet it is often viewed in such a manner, either by the advocates or the opponents of psychiatric involuntary treatment. The problem is for whom, for how long, at what stage and what kind of hospital. What might be the effects for the patient of being hospitalized for a month, a year or a ten year period? The data are inconclusive, but certainly not all research points to the inevitable development of the syndrome of institutionalization. (8) Obviously, answers to such complicated questions are hard to come by, but that does not take away from the validity of the question and should slow down those who readily accept Goffman's theories. (9)

Looking back historically on those who were considered mad and on the vicissitudes with which society approached and dealt with them, at times humanely, at times by sequestering or by exiling them, occasionally by ridicule, it is little wonder that the mad have inherited a tradition which is still part of their present-day image that they are potentially unpredictable and dangerous. Furthermore, society and the judicial system have accepted and the psychiatric profession attributes to them a distinct limitation in the exercise of their free will. It tends to be accepted that their behavior is under the duress of "mental disease" or "illness," so that they are unable to be held fully accountable for their acts and, at times, are judged to be incompetent and thus unable to exercise their inherent civil rights. Therefore, they have to be treated against their will because their will is actually diseased, and they have to be protected from the consequences of behavior arising from diseased intellect. They are at times held nonaccountable for criminal acts and judged as lacking in testamentary capacity.

Again, who were these people so judged in historical times as to be insane? Were they the ones that we would currently consider depressive or schizophrenic, or were these individuals primarily the retarded, the palsied and the malformed, those who as a result of genetic or early environmental factors were deficient in neurological coordination or intellectual development? In fact, knowing the cruelty of the middle ages and remembering that as recently as the 18th century mental hospitals were places that were visited by people who came to laugh at the antics of the mad, one wonders whether the architectural gargoyles on European buildings are expressions of what society at that time considered to be the lunatic. Extrapolating from that, one would be forced to conclude that the mad of those days were predominantly the physically and intellectually deformed, the mongoloid idiots, the cerebral palsied, the mentally retarded.

Yet, at the time of Edward, the English did differentiate the lunatic from the mentally retarded moron. (10) This difference led to a different form of safekeeping and of social intervention. Blackstone's commentaries on the judicial system seem to suggest that for many centuries a certain form of intervention akin to what we would now consider involuntary hospitalization was practiced in England. French literature also suggests a similar concern which resulted in the notorious and dreaded *lettres de cachets*. (11) The concern behind this intrusion on individual rights was primarily one of protecting family estate and family reputation and honor.

Treatment as such, when practiced, saw physicians of those days intervene in an aggressive manner, and their interventions must have been disastrous for many of their patients. The moral treatment of the 18th century, of which so much has been made, was basically a form of granting the mentally ill an asylum where they could rest and be treated decently and have a period of time (a moratorium) away from their worries and concerns. It is interesting that in a somewhat similar manner, socialist Poland (among others) has developed rest houses for many of its workers. These places are a combination of psychiatric asylums as we know them in the United States and the watering hole spas of central and western Europe. Nervous exhaustion and neurasthenia are the conditions which are appropriately referred for treatment in these institutions. In the medieval days, and even as late as the 19th century, the inducement of vomiting, blood-letting, plus the invention of various spinning chairs and other gadgets must have made many a patient, whose main problem was some form of hysterical neurasthenia, get better in a hurry. (12) One can speculate, therefore, that the pain, the discomfort and the placebo effect would also have had some significant therapeutic effect. On the other hand, those whose physical health or morbidity was more serious were most likely to fall prey to intercurrent infections and become institutionalized and die.

The brief clinical vignettes presented in these historical studies are interpolated with the current interpretations of facts. Yet, even though the specifics may very well be subject to historiographic criticism, what can very well be perceived is the constant struggle between the concern for the individual as opposed to the concern for his community and family and his responsibility and accountability to the king, the political system or religion. In medieval days, society took for granted — and accepted as normal and reasonable — the concept of torture as a necessary part in the inquisition of an accused individual. A plea of guilt obtained under such coercion, which conceivably led in major crimes to the stake, was considered reasonable since it saved the individual from himself and saved his soul... the most important part of man. Physicians who attributed these processes to a form of illness were not only, at times, out of step with the social or political thinking, but were perceived as dangerous and harmful to the individual because they jeopardized his immortal soul. (13) Currently, the mentally ill are also in the process of being protected on one hand by the civil libertarian who insists that society has to pay a price for the preservation of individual freedom and, on the other hand, by those within our own professional ranks who insist that he be treated (and, unfortunately, often maltreated) by the enthusiastic physician to save him from illness often only to push him back to that environment and style of life in which the patient was unable to cope. (14)

We still see the struggle between the protection of the community from those who are sick, deviant or antisocial and the protection of the individual. We still see in our society an inability to come to the ultimate resolution of how much is due the citizen and how much his community; what is the ultimate loyalty of that individual? Is it to his country or to his society, to his family or merely to his own inherent right of the pursuit of happiness?

Yet, it is this philosophical preoccupation with autonomy and allegiance which has consistently escaped comprehensive understanding and continually confounds our attempts to arrive at a meaningful concept of the determination of free will versus determinism and of social versus individual obligation. In medieval times, the king was considered to have divine right and the individual had one aim in life — the salvation of his immortal soul by allegiance to the king and church. From the king down, the aims of society, at least superficially, were in agreement with this single aim and sought to achieve it for every member. As we have become more philosophically developed, as we no longer attribute divine right to kings or even to our elected presidents, as the sanctity of marriage has become a contract which may have more or less meaning, as society has become a group of people to be manipulated by the advertiser on behalf of his client, credence can begin to be given to the possibility that maybe the mad are the only ones who are sane in our society.

It is rather difficult to find many references to regulations, law or precedents pertaining to the practice of the confinement and involuntary treatment of the mad or the mentally ill in the literature pertaining to the history of psychiatry. There are certain postulated principles, however, which, until quite recently, appeared to guide custom and society. Early Roman laws stated, "If a person is a fool, let this person and his goods be under the protection of his family or his paternal relatives, if he is not under the care of anyone." (15)

English jurisprudence appears to dictate that the lunatic became a ward of the king, and his person was taken care of by a conservator and his estate by a trustee, and the two roles were always separated, since one would do everything in his power to help the man (to recover) while the other would preserve the estate, since he would be the beneficiary in event of death. In

England in the 18th century, rules governing mad houses were promulgated. These mad houses were proprietary and most often nonmedically administered institutions. The early 18th century rules stated that only an individual who had been seen by a physician, surgeon, or apothecary and recommended for treatment in a mad house, could legitimately be held against his will. (16) This rule, however, did not pertain to the pauper or the indigent, and the local county or village authorities acting, presumably, in *parens patriae* philosophy, could put them in work houses at their own discretion. The role of the physician in adjudicating the need for treatment or custody of the poor did not apply until much later.

In Poland in 1791 rules were drawn up as part of the constitutional revamping which strictly regulated the rules and responsibilities for overseeing of the mentally ill, and which instituted a commission composed of citizens and physicians empowered to examine the relatives of the potential patient as well as his lifestyle. (17)

The English colonies in the northern American continent were very much influenced by the common law and traditions brought over from England, and again we had the same system of the pauper, the work houses, the asylums. Yet the tradition that the adult male member of the family disposed of his children as long as they were minor, and of his wife, pertained until the classic case of Mrs. Packard who eventually brought suit contending that her husband could not, at his whim and wish, hospitalize her in a mental asylum. (18)

It was the fact that we were dealing with people who were considered minor or, as it were, the property of others that, in many states, led to the probate judges being the adjudicators of the need for confinement. The development of the jury trial, which was advocated in English literature, which was redeveloped after the Packard trial and which, as recently as 1973 was affirmed as an inherent right by the American Psychiatric Association, was meant to protect some of the unique characteristics of individuality and civil liberties that have been prized as inherent in the Anglo-Saxon system of governments, and as reaffirmed by the United States Constitution. Furthermore, when hospitalization was custodial and treatment minimal, then due process protection was imperative.

Reviewing, on a rather superficial level, some of the developments in other countries, one sees practices which span the spectrum of development as outlined above. On one hand, there exists the most crass neglect of the mentally ill, who are more often than not completely abandoned, neglected or housed in jails; there are situations in which family members and physicians use their concern and "informed" judgment. On the other hand is, undoubtedly, the most highly developed and civilized approach of the current English system in which mental health tribunals represent both community as well as medical and legal interest and adjudicate the need for hospitalization. (19)

This outline of some of the historical highlights perhaps should also be seen in the context of the constant fundamental philosophical issues that have fascinated and confronted humanity. These have had to do with issues of autonomy and with the problems of where and how human motivation is determined. As the mad or the alienated became more differentiated from other deviant groups and as "mad doctors" became a speciality, so a controversy arose, in England at least, whether the mad were fit subjects for the philosopher or for the physician. This battle had already been fought in the social context, whether the mad were possessed by the devil and belonged to the inquisition or the clergy. Currently, no one is particularly concerned at the philosopher's being involved with the mentally ill, though perhaps a number of psychiatrists, with some justification in a small number of cases, might claim that the psychiatrist currently represents a very high level of philosophical expertise. It is the sociologist and the attorney who now make claim on the mentally ill, asserting that the patient is only a persecuted member of society and that society should be modified, arguing that the patient is deprived of his rights and should be protected from the aggressive psychiatrist-physician.

This question of nature versus nurture, of determinism versus free will continues to confound us. Opinion has been so recently polarized that it is difficult even in academic circles to talk about the inheritance of temperament, intelligence, personality, or potential for mental illness without being vehemently and emotionally attacked for ideological-repressive-racist and sexist attitudes. This attitude, perhaps taken to the nth degree, seems to assert that man is potentially perfect and has its tradition in the romantic writers of the 19th century who felt that humanity had within it a potential for good as long as it was steered and developed in the right direction. The profession of psychiatry is also caught in this web, since it is based on two different traditions: the healer and the scientist. On one hand, psychiatry attempts a scientific explanation for disease and has its roots in the tradition of 19th century medicine. The older tradition harks back to the mad doctors of the 19th and 18th centuries, to the alienists of this country's history and ultimately to its origins, a mixture of quackery, witch doctors and shamans. In its approach to mental illness, psychiatry is ambivalent, since it postulates a deterministic disease model, yet in its psychotherapeutic approach (a throw-back to the philosophers?) it argues for the possibility of change due to the free will of the patient.

The scientific revolution highlighted the disparity between psychiatry and medicine. As the etiology of organic illness became organic instead of merely humoral, as pathology became a science helping the clinician, the treatment more specific and successful and the results more predictable, so psychiatry fell by the wayside and became the "Cinderella" and custodian of medicine. Unfortunately, psychiatrists became frustrated and, in attempting to emulate their colleagues, forgot their traditional humanitarianism. This attempt to continue their medical identity by indulging in heroic therapeutics was arrested by the advent of the psychoanalytic movement when listening, once again, became a legitimate and respectable therapeutic skill.

Scientific medicine has, as its goal, the eradication of disease either through preventive measures or through the rational scientific application of therapeutic skills, and so the logical development in psychiatry has been the application of these same concepts to mental illness. If historically the asylums were havens for the sick and the inadequate, so also did they become places for custodial care of those whose psychosocial disabilities made them unable to adapt to the challenge of their everyday life. The challenge of the growing number of inmates and the inchoate but atavistic conviction in all European and European-derived civilizations that these problems were in fact medical led in growing ways to the application of treatability as a reasonable condition for admission.

Historically, however, only those who had been unable to take care of themselves and who were charges to the family or to the local community were allowed to seek refuge in these havens. The legal profession also accepted *the principle* that the dangerous should be confined. Yet the 19th century saw the emergence of what has been described by some with pride and by some with derision as the therapeutic state. Treatability rather than dangerousness became a reasonable and accepted condition for admission to psychiatric asylums. In 1845 Judge Shaw of the Supreme Court of the State of Massachusetts, ruling on a case brought for habeas corpus by one Josiah Oakes who argued that he had been illegally committed by his family, held that Oakes had been lawfully committed and made a ruling which is still in the United States the foundation for many of the commitment laws as well as the bone of acrimony between the psychiatric profession and many attorneys:

> The right to restrain an insane person of his liberty is found in that great law of humanity which makes it necessary to confine those who going at large would be dangerous to themselves or to others. And the necessity which creates the law creates the limitations of the law. The question must then arise in each particular case whether a patient's own safety, or that of others, requires that he should be restrained for a certain time, and whether restraint is necessary for his restoration, or will be conductive thereto. The restraint can continue as long as the necessity continues. This is the limitation and the proper limitation. (20)

As is the case in many court decisions, it neither became accepted by all nor did it represent necessarily a unanimous concensus. Neither was it a new innovation, because for many years prior to that ruling physicians committed patients to hospitals on a mere scribbled signature with a statement that

John Doe is a fit subject for confinement in the asylum. (21) That "fit subject" concept represents a potential variety of both innovative and progressive ideas as well as of intellectual, medical and legal ineptitude. The decision, however, reflected a judicial sanction of a practice that had been under way in America and in Europe for many years, if not centuries. The decision, therefore, reinforced the application of this practice and of this philosophy.

We know that the legal profession has always postulated free will, but then has made exceptions for the individuals who are immature, who are morons or who are under the influence of duress of mental illness. In the past, this autonomy was thought to be invaded by supernatural influences. In the era of scientific medicine, this duress was regarded as being due to inherent genetic, degenerative disorder. Hence, the early name for one of these conditions, dementia praecox. Currently, the autonomy is regarded as being affected by social forces.

Ultimately, in the current social and legal context, the issue of autonomy also involves issues of informed consent, a point which goes way beyond the boundaries of mental illness and of psychiatrists specifically, but begins to affect all patients in general. It is hard to know at what point reasonable informed consent is a legitimate and fundamental issue and at which point it becomes unreasonable. (22)

Yet, we have proceeded to a stage of medical and scientific development where behavior modification, psychosurgery, even milieu therapy are both effective and, at the same time, legitimately raise the fear of the state imposing its own values on its citizens. (23) Yet it is here in this area that the battle is joined. The medical man argues that society has empowered him with a mandate and his training has prepared him to exercise this mandate of treating the ill. Surely once a procedure is underway no physician in his right mind continually explains the step by step technique or, for that matter, questions the level of voluntariness of a patient midway in the treatment.

The attorney falls back on the question of informed consent. In the famous words of John Stuart Mill:

> The only purpose for which power can be rightfully exercised over any member of a civilized community, against his will, is to

prevent harm to others. His own good, either physical or moral is not a sufficient warrant.

The attorney questions whether any one for any cause has the right to deprive a citizen of freedom without due process. Furthermore, many attorneys question the existence of "mental illness" and whether therapy is anything but a coercion of society to modify attitudes and a scientific progressive form of thought and attitude control.

Hence, the issue is joined!

NOTES

1. The classic book by Robert Burton, *The Anatomy of Mlancholia*, London, 1660, is certainly crucial in the development of the social approach to the perception of mental derangements as opposed to the medieval concept of possession. The reader is referred to any of the works on history of psychiatry for assessment of this treatise. (See note 5). Yet the passions of jealousy described do not translate readily into our current thinking of depression. R. Hunter and I. MacAlpine's book, *Three Hundred Years of Psychiatry, 1535-1860*, Oxford University Press, London, 1963, is an excellent compendium of historical psychiatry from the time of the Renaissance to the middle of the Victorian era. The authors comment on the fact that in England in the 16th century, in addition to the surgeons company, the apothecaries, and the graduate physicians, a fourth group of practitioners existed and was licensed by the Diocesan Bishops, instituted by an Act of Parliament of 1511, at the time of Henry VIII. This recognized two specialists, those pursuing 1) midwifery and 2) the treatment of the lunatic. It is interesting that this early form of psychiatry was recognized as a specialty under the term of "Practice on the Melancholy and Mad." It is clear the melancholia was recognized as a specific form of mental illness but not necessarily perceived in the same way that we see depression nowadays. On the other hand, we are not much better off currently, since the word "depression" tends to be loosely used, to describe people who are sad, unhappy, frustrated or psychotically depressed.

2. A number of different studies have addressed themselves to the problem of normality, but by far the most comprehensive is: D. Offer, and M. Sabshin, *Normality: Theoretical and Clinical Concepts of Mental Health.* (New York, Basic Books, Inc., 1966). The problem of normality as it affects the mentally ill person is obviously the bone of contention in this area. Joseph J. O'Connell's "The Medical-legal aspects of Insanity, with reference to Commitments, Jury Trials and Expert Testimony," *Medical News of New York*, 454-461 (1897), makes this telling point: "I have often had the question, 'what is insanity?' asked

me in court and have heard it many times propounded to my professional a
sociates . . . but each and every time I have heard the definition picked apart in the
cross examination by a cunning lawyer." O'Connell then quotes Boileau, "All
men are insane, but some are able to hide it better than others" and Montesquie,
"Insane asylums were built in order that the outside world would consider itself
sane." In 1973 the A.P.A. formed a committee to define the concept of mental
illness.

3. The literature in this area is comprehensive, and only a sample of the writings
can be suggested. Among these the following studies deserve specific
recognition: J. P. Leff, "Culture and the Differentiation of Emotional States,"
British Journal of Psychiatry, 123: 299-307 (1973). J. C. Carothers, "A Study of
Mental Derangement in Africans and an Attempt to Explain its Peculiarities
more especially in Relation to the African Attitude to Life," *Psychiatry*, XI: 47-
81 (1948). E. D. Wittkower, H. B. Murphy, J. Fried, and H. Ellenberger, "Cross
Cultural Inquiry into the Symptomatology of Schizophrenia," *Annals of the
New York Academy of Sciences*, LXXXIV: 851-863 (1960).

4. The standard, *Diagnostic and Statistical Manual of Mental Disorders,* Second
Edition, (DSM-II), American Psychiatric Association, Washington, D.C., 1968,
is based on the diagnostic nosology initially developed by Krepelin at the end of
the 19th century. The DSM-II was originally developed during the Second
World War to facilitate the understanding and description of the behavior of
inducted personnel who came to the attention of the authorities and, often, of the
military psychiatrists. Recently modified (1968) to conform more closely to the
World Health Organization international standards, it (International
Classification of Disease) still is a constantly flexible guideline modified by new
data and attitudes. As recently as 1974 saw a challenge to one of the accepted
diagnostic terms — namely, homosexuality. The A.P.A. Board of Trustees in
December 1973 *ruled* that homosexuality be changed from a subcategory of
sexual deviation with fetishism, pedophilia, transvestism (category of
personality and nonpsychotic mental disorders) to sexual orientation
disturbance. *Psychiatric News*, IX:2 (1974).
   Many psychiatrists who, in addition to their basic three years of residency have
pursued analytic training, use concepts and labels derived purely from Freudian
analytic psychology. It is not unusual for one medical center to freely use a
concept such as "hysterical psychoses" which cannot be found in any standard
text and which is not in the A.P.A. nomenclature. Another medical center may,
on the other hand, freely use the concept of "borderline psychoses." I do not
mean to imply that these two conditions are the same, but merely to point out
that such discrepancies occur. A specific research project between the United
States and Britain also showed marked changes in the pattern of diagnosing
mental illness: R. E. Kendell, et al., "Diagnostic Criteria of American and British
Psychiatrists," *Archives of General Psychiatry*, 25:123-130 (1970).
   This does not necessarily imply, as is suggested by some critics of psychiatry,

that all mental illness is culturally determined or culturally perceived. When criteria are uniformly developed and uniformly applied, the diagnostic categories of mental illness such as schizophrenia tend to follow statistically similar patterns in developed, undeveloped and developing countries. For the latest research on this see World Health Organization: *The International Pilot Study of Schizophrenia,* Geneva, 1973.

5. The English language has seen a number of excellent books on the history of psychiatry. The classic by which most are judged is: Zilboorg and G. W. Henry, *A History of Medical Psychology* (New York, Norton, 1941). A more modern and more succinctly written text is: G. Rosen, *Madness in Society* (London, Keegan, Paul, 1968).

6. The literature on schizophrenia is so voluminous that it defies any simple unbiased summary. Undoubtedly, prejudice is shown, but for the most up-to-date viewpoint on this disorder one should refer to: D. Rosenthal, and S. Kety, *Transmission of Schizophrenia* (London, Pergamon, 1968), also T. Lidz, *The Origin and Treatment of Schizophrenic Disorders* (New York, Basic Books, 1973) and L. Bellak, and L. Loeb, *The Schizophrenic Syndrome* (New York, Grune & Stratton, 1969).

7. It appears that the overview in introductory courses which are the main staple for many American college students tends to simplify complex problems. The European university student (a graduate of the gymnasium) reads a very concentrated and specific subject. He either pursues sociology or political science, etc., and by and large realizes his shortcomings and ignorance in areas outside of his courses. Many of the graduates of European universities have justifiably been perceived by Americans as trained rather than educated. On the other hand, one of the problems of the American college graduate is that he appears to have had contact with many different aspects of knowledge, but basically grasps very few of the principles behind any of them.

8. W. R. Gove, and T. Fain, "The Stigma of Mental Hosptialization: An Attempt to Evaluate the Consequences," *Archives of General Psychiatry,* 28:494-500 (1973).

9. E. Goffman, *Asylums* (Chicago, Aldine Press, 1961).

10. This point is elucidated in Sir William Blackstone's *Commentaries on the Laws of England.* 1765-9, Oxford-Clarendon Press and quoted in Hunter and MacAlpine (cf. fn. 1). Blackstone writes that, according to old English common law, there were two groups of mentally ill: the idiots from birth, "a nativitate," and lunatics of "non compos mentis." According to Blackstone's commentaries, the old common law affirmed by parliamentary statute at the time of Edward II, the Lord Chancellor exercised protection over both these groups on behalf of the

King. However, a jury of twelve had to make this decision. This appears to be a very early development of what was recreated in American jurisprudence in the 19th century, namely of mandating a peer decision as to a legal/medical status of a citizen. It is difficult not to interpret from the writings of Blackstone that the jury trial was to protect an individual from being hospitalized. However, in fairness, this is not a conclusive assertion.

11. H. Baruk, "Internement, Interdiction et Curatelle: Necessite D'eviter le Retour a L'arbitraire a Propos des Lois Sur les Incapables," *Bulletin Academie Nat'l Medicine,* 150:41-44 (1966).

12. The forms of treatment in psychiatry varied from the most up-to-date to the most bizarre and even brutal. Bleeding, inducement of vomiting, catharsis, were all too frequently used. However, as medicine in general became more treatment-oriented and began to develop specific forms of intervention for various symptomatological entities, so did the variety of interventions that were developed to treat the mentally ill or the insane. Spinning chairs, ducking into cold water were all tried and all had their specific enthusiastic advocates. In particular see: A. Deutsch, *The Mentally Ill in America* (New York, Columbia University Press, 1969).

13. There is, at times, an assumption that the sophisticated approach to the understanding and the treatment of the mentally ill followed a generally ascending scientific level of sophistication comparable to man's understanding of sciences in general and also paralleled in the advances of general medicine. However, it is quite obvious from reading the literature that, at any given time, there were marked ambivalences and continued vicissitudes in the approach to the understanding of the mentally ill. The 16th century was the time of the progressive Johan N. Weyher (becoming known as the founder of modern psychiatry), but also the era of the father of modern surgery, Ambroise Pare, who urged his royal master to execute all witches, quoting the biblial injunction, "Thou Shalt not Suffer a Witch to live." The age of moral treatment in the 18th century was followed by the tragic abuses described in the reports of the Madhouse Commission in the 19th century. Hunter and MacAlpine, (cf. fn. 1). In 1812 Benjamin Rush advocated: "for refractory patients pouring cold water under the sleeve, so that it may descend into the armpits and down the trunk of the body." *Medical Inquiries and Observations upon Diseases of the Mind* (Philadelphia, Kimber, Richardson, 1812).

14. The New York Civil Liberties' Union in their legislative memorandum No. 1 which was given some publicity by being printed in the *Psycho-Analytic Review,* 58:385-394 (1971), makes no bones that the issue is one of ideological rather than pragmatic approach. The impassioned document, of course, includes the classical case of the Justice Robert Jackson who, following a heart attack, continued to function as a Justice of the Supreme Court in spite of his

physician's advice to retire and thus jeopardized his life — an argument so palpably illogical as not to be worth further refutation. The document concludes with the statement that "abolition of involuntary confinement would cause much human degradation and social harm"; however, they go on to qualify it by stating the following: "but less, PERHAPS (capitalizations are the author's) than its retention." The ACLU takes a very ideological position, and again the mentally ill are not being protected — they are being sacrificed for the sake of alleged freedoms of the rest of society. This point, one of the focal criticisms of the involuntary commitment process, will be elaborated further in Chapter V. Intellectual honesty, however, demands that the inchoate thinking of physicians in this area has to be recognized. Peszke and Wintrob in the study "Emergency Commitment — A Transcultural Study," *Journal of American Psychiatry*, 131:36-40 (1974), documented well the nearly cavalier approach of the average psychiatrist to the mentally ill and to his own professional medical narcissism. Such remarks as, "When in doubt, hospitalize" or "I act in the interest of the patients and I'm responsible in every case in my practice."

Also, the point was made in 19th century England by Dr. James Stephen that insanity for an attorney means conduct of a certain degree while for a physician it means a disease.

15. W. J. Curran, "Hospitalization of the Mentally Ill" *North Carolina Law Review, 31:*274-298 (1967).

16. W. S. S. Maclay, "The New Mental Health Act in England and Wales" *American Journal of Psychiatry, 116:*777-781 (1960), and James Parkinson: "Mad Houses, Observations on the act regulating mad houses, etc." in Hunter and MacAlpine (cf. fn. 1). Original magistrate commitment of 1714 modified by a physician's certificate in 1774. Parkinson suggested "an authorized arbitrator" which in 1959 saw the Mental Health Tribunal. But prior to that, England passed the 1845 Act "for the regulation and Treatment of Lunatics." Also only a licensed house or hospital could hold the insane to prevent social harm.

17. M. Lyskanowski, "Methods of dealing with the Mentally Ill during the 18th century in Poland," *Psychiatria polska, 3:*203-206 (1969).

18. R. Dewey, "The Jury Law for Commitment of the Insane in Illinois, 1867-1893" and Mrs. E.P.W. Packard, "Later Developments in the Lunacy Legislation in Illinois," *American Journal of Insanity, 69:*571-584 (1913).

19. J. C. Wood, "Mental Health Review Tribunals," *Medical Science and Law,* 7:86-92 (1971).

20. Both A. Deutsch, *The Mentally Ill in America,* supra note 12, as well as N. N. Kittrie, *The Right to be Different* (Baltimore, Johns Hopkins Press, 1972) discuss this problem from slightly different historical and philosophical

viewpoints.

21. Deutsch, supra notes 12 and 20, makes reference to the informality of admitting an individual to an asylum during the early days of this country. A couple of scribbled words on a piece of paper to the effect that "an individual is a proper patient for the hospital" were sufficient.

22. The constant question is the necessary amount of information and knowledge that a patient needs from his physician. In formed consent tends to have three aspects: complete knowledge, competence to make a decision and finally, freedom of choice or voluntariness. Physicians readily make statements that it is difficult to explain the benefits of an operative or medical treatment to a patient who is consumed by anxiety, pain or apprehension and who wishes to be helped rather than to be terrorized psychologically by the various possible harmful side effects of the procedure. If each of these points is analyzed, medical practice is challenged at every step. To urge a patient to comply with a therapeutic regime which may turn out to be harmful can be interpreted as psycholgoical coercion by an authoritarian physician.

Any patient with an emotional problem could raise the issue of competence. This situation will probably lead to very vexing law suits and, as so much in this area, the price to society may outweigh its benefits.

23. See J. Robitscher "Psychosurgery and other Somatic Means of Altering Behavior," *Bulletin of the American Academy of Psychiatry and the Law, 2:*7-33 (1974).

CHAPTER II

THE MEDICAL TRADITION AND
SCOPE OF THE PROBLEM

Looking over the historical perspective, one is confronted by the fact that society always differentiated between behavior caused by evil (legal concept of mens rea) and sickness or possession. The first fell into the category of criminal law and was to be punished, and the second within the province of the healer. It is difficult to understand some of the logic behind such a division, and it may not necessarily be compatible with our own 20th century differentiation of criminal behavior (antisocial) from mental illness or disorder. Yet intuitively, society — or at least western European society — had no trouble making such a distinct separation. This does not imply that the attitudes or reactions of society to those considered mentally ill were necessarily more humane or therapeutic, but it is a fact that there was a strong current of thinking, of attitude and of feeling that some individuals need to be punished and condemned, some to be treated and pitied.

Virchov, in a very perceptive way, stated that "physicians of other centuries have been the attorneys and the caretakers of the poor." (1) When the profession of medicine was less scientific, when it was closer to the healing religious fraternities and in the collective perception of society identified with the witch doctors or the shamans, then it was logical and reasonable for the physician to be involved with a whole host and wide spectrum of human miseries and sufferings. Even in the advanced, cynical and materialistic second part of the 20th century, there are still numbers of physicians who have embarked on missionary work of different kinds, and such names as Dr. Schwietzer, Dr. Doolittle, the American ship "Hope" and the Peace Corps physicians document the altruism of many in the profession.

Physicians accepted as their province the mandate to relieve suffering, to imbue with hope, to help the anguished. Society had no difficulty in perceiving that whatever the etiological basis, whether organic or environmental, there were people who were anguished, in pain, suffered despair and needed help. The modern day critics who state that the medical profession has monopolized the care of the sick and excluded other disciplines which are as competent or more so in delivering care ignore the fact that medicine did not start with the A.M.A. or the medical schools or even with Hippocrates, but has existed as a reaction to distress!

Such were the beginnings of the medical tradition in the treatment of the mentally ill. It was, furthermore, strengthened by the 19th century scientific breakthroughs in medicine and the realization that many forms of particularly prevalent mental illness were caused by biological factors. Myxedema due to hypothyroidism was not perceived for many centuries as an endocrinological disorder, but only diagnosed when incapacitating mental symptoms had developed. General paralysis of the insane, one of the advanced stages of syphilitic infection, was also only pathologically differentiated by medical scientists in the 19th century, and its infectious origins elicited with specific treatment more or less successfully applied.

Medicine in the last hundred years has made tremendous breakthroughs and psychiatry has also made certain significant accomplishments.

In England some of the mental hospitals, the places for the mad, had been run as nonprofessional money-making institutions (akin to some of the proprietary ambulance companies that still exist in the United States), but in the North American continent the asylums became medical institutions and their superintendents were actually both the experts in the area of mental health and also united to form the core of a body which in time became the American Psychiatric Association. Again, it is difficult to document the specific thinking behind this development except the intuitive conviction of society that these people — fit subjects for confinement as many statutes read — were in need of a help which only the medical profession had the tradition, the wisdom and the humanitarian interest to assume.

Social work, psychology had yet to develop. The organized religious orders were already defunct, and the legal profession had still 100 years to go before it discovered its interest in the mentally ill.

The concerns of society were also different in the middle 1800's as opposed to the middle 1900's. At that time treatment was custodial, the results discouraging and perverse, cures unpredictable. No wonder that society also developed an attitude that only those who showed forms of dangerousness to themselves or to their community should be involuntarily incarcerated. Since treatment had little chance of success, the unfortunate idiosyncratic person was just as well off in society at large as he was locked in the asylum.

On the other hand, for many people the asylum was exactly what its named signified — a place away from the stresses of life, a haven where food and a certain level of creature comforts were provided at a social price of regression — "instutitionalization" — where social and family demands were minimal, where regression was tolerated and, in fact, the asylum was for some — particularly the inadequate — a perfectly desirable place in which to live. This is still the case for many, (2) so much so that many states made voluntary admissions to these institutions impossible or very difficult, and, in a review of the commitment and psychiatric admission policies to state institutions, the GAP Committee in 1948 inferred that probably financial reasons were the main problem preventing many states from allowing voluntary admissions. (3) The legislatures were concerned that their hard-pressed, understaffed, inadequately financed institutions would be swamped by people wishing to obtain admission and a free meal ticket! Yet scientific breakthroughs in psychiatric methodology and treatment began to prevail and excite interest as well as raise hope for the future. The physician, in general, became much more identified with a scientific biological tradition. The physician pursuing psychiatry as a specialty began to have a choice of one of two paths: either the organic treatment and custodial approach or the analytical psychotherapeutic, usually office-based practice. Both tended to over-elaborate the scientific basis of psychiatric practice as far as the knowledge of that date is concerned and tended to minimize the tradition of humanitarianism and case work. Progressively, more of what had been done by physicians in the past became delegated to the nurses, social workers and even the Red Cross. (In a recent advertisement on the radio for the American Red Cross the point was made that the Red Cross has involved itself in care-taking in relation to problems which no other group wishes to or is able to manage. They are involved with, among others, the help to the victims of floods, the teaching of the blind and the deaf, instructions in swimming and first-aid, health education in schools...a whole variety of socially important and relevant issues with which medicine of the 20th century is too sophisticated to concern itself and which even social work has, at this point, abandoned as not falling within its professional identity.)

Psychiatric treatment continued to be innovative and, at times, to raise the most serious social concerns. The originator of the lobotomy, Dr. Moniz, won a Nobel Prize for this procedure in 1949 (first done in 1936). Twenty such interventions saw the government of Portugal stop it. More recently, of course, psychosurgery has also raised serious issues. (4) Electric-convulsive therapy had a major therapeutic effectiveness, particularly in depressed patients, but also was abused by many practitioners. The invention of the major antipsychotic medications in the middle 1950's was perhaps the most significant and therapeutic breakthrough and led to an emptying of the chronic wards of state facilities in this country as well as in Europe. It gave hope that psychiatry could, indeed, be therapeutically effective. Psychiatry certainly felt that it had made a major breakthrough and perhaps overextended its goals as well as exaggerated its accomplishments. Various voices were raised for psychiatry to become socially relevant, to restructure the whole phase of society; psychiatrists were exhorted to become involved in problems of racial inequity, to resolve international tensions, and to diagnose and remedy social ills. (5) Many considered it quite reasonable to become as active in the treatment of those who are called by our society the socially deviant and criminal as with those who suffer from psychic problems. It is rather paradoxical that we are now facing an attempt by many attorneys to see issues of mental illness as a variation of the criminal process, while only twenty years ago psychiatrists felt that issues of criminal process should be seen as psychiatric issues!

One of the most eminent psychiatrists has suggested public health measures for mental illness akin to those of other medical organic problems. (6) The complete discreditation of organized religion which had to become involved in social services to continue its existence, led many to seek individual counselling and a search for personal identity and a meaningful life on psychiatric couches. This tended to identify many nearly normal people as mentally ill and, furthermore, it raised an issue of empathy for the mentally ill in those who, at times, experience self-doubt, unhappiness or anxiety.

Perhaps the height of the ridiculous grandiosity and the lack of any professional restraint was the tremendous response of American psychiatrists to an invitation by a newspaper in 1964 to write their opinions about Goldwater's emotional stability and suitableness for the Presidency. (7) Over 4,000 responses were sent in, highlighting both the naivete of many in the profession as well as the fact that their own political and ideological perceptions were clouding their professional judgment. It is imperative to keep this in mind because the psychiatric profession is *not the only one* in which *political and ideological values cloud professional judgment or influence professional decision*. The same holds true for law, sociology, and social work. In that particular case, however, it led to a very responsive condemnation by the A.P.A. of such behavior and to a quick realization on the part of many psychiatrists that, indeed, objectivity was not infinite. Seymour Halleck documented some of these problems very well in his excellent book. (8) Yet the conviction in the mind of the physician-psychiatrist that the mentally ill were to be treated because they were ill and psychiatry had the means to cure them continues to be the prevalent mode of professional thinking and attitude and still shows no signs of ebbing. (9) This may not necessarily in itself be a criticism of the psychiatric profession, but it does lead to problems when one looks at the diagnostic manual where many forms of behavior are categorized as mental disorders. (10)

This manual lists a whole variety of conditions, reactions, attitudes and life styles and, while some may, indeed, be factually and even physically diagnosable as organic brain syndrome due to epilepsy and while many may have a high degree of diagnosable reliability and respond to treatment such as acute schizophrenic reactions, there are a variety of categories that raise serious criticism as well as serious questions. We find such conditions as personality disorders, e.g., obsessive-compulsiveness. When one looks at the history of this nomenclature, there is some rhyme and reason to it. It was developed by military psychiatrists as a way of categorizing behavior to judge compatibility with military service, accepted by the Veterans' Administration as a way of categorizing behavior that is pensionable as service-connected disability and then assumed by the American Psychiatric Association which, having a strong analytic orientation, found it helpful as a shorthand way of communication. However, as it developed it became abused, and in the famous and often quoted case from St. Elizabeth's a decision was handed down by the Superintendent stating that personality disorders are a form of mental illness. (11)

It is difficult to justify such thinking, and reaction was predictable.

With the growth of psychiatric empire building occurred the tremendous growth of the National Institutes of Mental Health and the propagation of community mental health clinics under the Kennedy-sponsored bill; a whole variety of innovative trends continued to be manifest, but at the same time, the legal profession began to be concerned, become involved, and found a cause celebre. Some of the practices became challenged: the inadequacy of treatment in state facilities, problems with forced labor of state hospital inmates, concerns about the battle of the experts in insanity trials and the tragedy of inmates held in institutions for many decades pending trial on the grounds of their alleged incompetence aroused justifiable anger. Accusations were hurled that psychiatry functions in the dark, behind the scenes and that the profession is afraid of being scrutinized. (12)

Mavericks arose within the profession itself who denied the existence of mental illness and who asserted that the profession was an agent of the establishment, attempting to coerce the general public to adopt uniform and middle class standards of behavior. Coincidental and influenced by the racial inequities in the United States, there was an overemphasis on the cultural, environmental factors determining behavior. (13) This in turn led to downgrading of the biological spects as an explanation for racial behavior and for maladaptive regression. The downgrading of the biological predictably led to the criticism of psychiatry and a reaction to the medical model and tradition. Psychiatry became described as having "imputed" knowledge rather than professional competence. (14)

There seems little doubt that the profession is guilty of some or, in part, of all of the criticisms. The trend in practice and criticism is not uniform, and the problem certainly tends to fluctuate. (15) It is being challenged in courts as well as being faced within the medical profession. There is little doubt that for many decades organized psychiatry had been scandalously unconcerned with those who are the sickest in the population, namely, those who are hospitalized in state institutions. These institutions were allowed to develop into snake pits, were understaffed and the worse-trained and the least-competent physicians tended to work in them. (16) It is also rather interesting that a perusal of the psychiatric literature in the 1950's and 1960's fails to elicit any guidelines to the practicing physician or psychiatrist as to the criteria for the use of involuntary hospitalization. (17)

The current issue has to do with the medical model which takes for granted that the sick should be treated and which considers mental illness as a disease. The opposite view negates the entity of mental illness or, at its most constructive, accepts the possibility that there is a need for involuntary treatment, but wishes to emphasize the protection of the individual by recourse to the legal profession's scrutiny. Furthermore, the medical model argues that the ill have a moral right to treatment and that civilization is measured as much by the humaneness to the sick as by education of the children.

I have, as it were, polarized the problem between two different attitudes. Unfortunately, there is a considerable amount of misunderstanding and of distortion of these conflicting positions. Often ideological and political attitudes contaminate basic ignorance of the problem or of the concern so that these issues of principle (confusing anyway) become presented and advocated in a biased, dialectical way which tends to denigrate the concern of opposite opinion and to precipitate acrimony rather than a search for the most pragmatic and reasonable compromise. In fact, one is confronted by the view that compromise is dangerous.

The problem is highlighted, furthermore, by certain secondary medical and legal issues which flow directly from the basic issue that those who are mentally ill and unable to seek treatment have to be committed. Is the medical emergency certificate or, for that matter, the probate judges' or magistrates' commitment for involuntary treatment tantamount to the use of any or all forms of treatment? Thus, is the confinement of a patient on the basis of medical judgment because that patient's serious mental state is interfering with his welfare tantamount to a sanction to use injections of tranquilizing medication? Does that entitle the receiving hospital to use electric shock therapy, or does it possibly entitle such a treatment center to perform psychosurgery? (18) Within these parameters of progressively greater and more heroic interventions are forms of treatment which superficially are harmless but which raise philosophical issues that are just as troublesome. (19) Milieu therapy, which is currently one of the most common and popular forms of treatment in the majority of inpatient psychiatric units, has as its premise the fact that "the group" in some ways determines and directs by its approval and consensus, yet this obviously tends to psychologically coerce a patient towards approved forms of behavior. It is but a small step from a milieu therapy unit to behavior modification, in which patients are presented clearly with certain goals, and progress in that direction is rewarded while, on the other hand, social and psychological punishments are devised for behavior which is not accepted by the staff or compatible with the goals of the institution.

These different problems tend to be illustrative of the difficulty faced by society, the medical profession and those who are concerned about abuses of individual rights in the treatment of the mentally ill.

Having outlined some of the highlights of these issues, let me describe some of the actual problems in detail. *For the physician, the patient who comes for help deserves treatment, and if he needs treatment the physician has a moral and an inherent medical obligation to provide such treatment to the best of his ability.* It may sound simplistic and to many critics of the medical-psychiatric profession even "corny," yet the physician feels that mental illness is no different from any other form of disease and that treatment should be as aggressive and comprehensive as is the treatment of heart failure, a bleeding peptic ulcer or hypertension. The physician takes the position that while in the case of a patient suffering from concussion or epileptic seizure state the emergency intervention is a common sense and legally mandated necessity, so the issue of patients' informed consent or of permission for treatment does not arise. And, indeed, in fact, this is not merely a medical attitude, but one which has found support in courts and which is established in many centuries of medical practice. (20) A patient who arrives in an emergency room following an accident and who is either seriously hurt or unconscious as a result of his injuries will not be abandoned pending the signature to some slip of paper in which he agrees to treatment. He or she is treated and, at times, surgically operated upon, the body assaulted with tubes, needles and other medical and laboratory procedures. The windpipe may be cut for a life-saving tracheostomy; the skull may be opened to relieve pressure from internal bleeding; tubes may be stuck into various orifices of the body and medications applied — all of this purely at the judgment of the physician or physicians in attendance. No one, basically, would challenge the fact that in such situations medical judgment has to be expeditiously applied to save life and that the issue of informed consent is basically not applicable.

We begin to get into more difficult ethical and problematical areas when we consider the alcoholic arrested on the streets in acute delirium tremens who, instead of being thrown into jail, is brought by an understanding and progressive police force to the emergency room for treatment. The drunken patient has brought his condition on himself, has not sought help, but is experiencing definite psychological and physiological manifestations which, without treatment, in a significant percentage of cases, will lead to exhaustion, probable heart failure and even possible death. (21)

For many physicians, mental illness fits the same model. The acute schizophrenic in his acute anxiety is perceived by the physician in exactly the same way as the two other examples given above. Let me, however, present for some discussion and thought a number of cases from my actual experience of mental illness and let us see whether they follow the medical model and whether intervention is justified.

It is not unusual in an emergency room of a large urban hospital to have the following situation. The police, on the complaint of a family member, arrive in a household to find a young male obviously experiencing auditory hallucinations, behaving in a very agitated and bizarre fashion with posturing and various facial mannerisms, talking in broken sentences with hard to understand speech, using obviously made-up words and expressing ideas which, in their bizarreness, would be amusing if the whole situtaion were not so obviously tragic. The family begs for help, may give a story that the young man has been progressively more withdrawn, isolated, preoccupied with his own fantasies, thoughts and problems, that he has stopped attending school, has begun to spend considerable number of hours in meditations and that the reason for the police being called was that the patient went through the house breaking all electronic objects and accusing the family of controlling his behavior by means of various electronic and electric devices.

The family does not wish the young man taken to jail, and the police also realize that they have a "psycho" on their hands and therefore take him to the emergency room. The physicians in the emergency room realize that this is a psychiatric problem and the psychiatrist on call examines and diagnoses the patient as an acute schizophrenic reaction. The physician considers the diagnosed mental illness to be a situation in which the cognitive and affective functioning of this individual is impaired in as significant a manner as would be the case of a concussion or "status epilepticus." Therefore, medical intervention is considered to be a sine qua non and, since the patient is acutely mentally ill, he is confined in a psychiatric unit or detained in the emergency room against his will for his own welfare. The average physician would consider the intervention of an attorney at this state as inappropriate as the presence of an attorney during the treatment of an internal cranial hemorrhage. It is a medical problem, since a medical diagnosis has been established which necessitates medical intervention.

Most progressive civilizations and legislatures provide for such medical intervention. While some make it very easy and some tend to make it exceedingly difficult, the fact of the matter is that in all the states of the union and in all the countries of Europe, the legal system sanctions the physician's hospitalizing such a patient against his will. For the physician, the hospitalization is only the first step in the process of treatment, and the extent and form of treatment that is then applied as well as the kind of diagnostic tests that may be performed to develop the diagnosis are purely matters of medical judgement. The patient is expected to submit to an electroencephalograph, and he may be encouraged or pressured into participating in various forms of psychological evaluations. Tranquilizing medicines are used profusely, by injection, if necessary. Restraints are applied, visiting restricted.

All of these steps are done to protect the patient and, in more recent years, the hospital and the staff from law suit. Again, informed consent is not sought, since one can hardly commit someone against his will and then assume that this same patient will agree to certain procedures. Furthermore, it appears to be paradoxical to assume that someone who is so sick that society, through the intervention of the medical man, needs to intervene on his behalf is in a position to give such informed consent.

To the physician the kind of treatment which he undertakes is purely and solely a matter of medical judgment. But, at this point, even for the acutely schizophrenic, even for that individual for whom hospitalization is seen by all and sundry as being necessary and as being therapeutic and in the society's and individual's best interest, the treatment is no longer so readily left to the judgment of the physician.

Few question the advisability or necessity of using various forms of sedatives or tranquilizing medications in treating the acutely distraught. But the unrestricted and uncontrolled use of seclusion rooms, physical restraints, and electric-convulsive treatment and the possibility of psychosurgery raise serious problems. Milieu therapy is so benign in its aspects that it also has somehow escaped critics, but behavior modification has certainly — even within the medical profession — raised the most serious ethical concerns. (22) But it is psychosurgery, a permanent surgical invasion and insult to the integrity of the brain and thus of the person and of his affect and his psyche, that has led to the mose vehement and vociferous outcry against uncontrolled treatment of the mentally ill. The court decision ruled that psychosurgery could not be performed on anyone who was involuntarily committed because informed consent could not be elicited. As has been argued by David Wexler, the decision of the Michigan court to prohibit psychosurgical intervention on an allegedly willing patient was well ruled on wrong grounds. (23) Certainly, it opens up the possibility that the stage of involuntary commitment may and should become separated from the stage of enforced treatment.

I have described a psychiatric problem which would, in all likelihood, not raise serious opposition or outcry except from such extremists as Szasz. It would be accepted by most that for the sake of the young man involuntary commitment was necessary, appropriate, and justified on legal, medical and ethical grounds. Let me present some situations which happen with frequency and which illustrate the scope of the problem, but in which the dispositions become more troublesome. Let us look at those cases in which the issue of mental illness, as such, is not at stake, but in which the disposition or problem of automony is at stake!

> A patient is brought to the emergency room, having been arrested following a physical assault on his family. He is in his 50's; history is given of progressively greater impairment of judgment in social decorum and business dealings; interpersonal frictions have been commented on by different members of the community; the family physician has made

recommendations that the man seek psychiatric treatment —
advice which was spurned; the wife has progressively and more
strongly given indications that she would no longer tolerate
such behavior, but would separate, and has already made
attempts to protect her own financial interests from the
patient's spendthrift activities. The assault was provoked by the
wife's stating that she would no longer stay in the same house
and submit to the husband's verbal, physical and sexual abuse
and molestation.

As we see the developments in some legislatures, this man could
only be arrested for criminal misconduct and would then be
charged. If he were charged with such criminal conduct, then
presumably the possibility of intervention of some kind would
exist. The individual, through his attorney, would raise the issue
of competency to stand trial or plead psychiatric illness as
exculpating his criminal conduct. However, assuming that the
disposition of this case followed a situation which would have
been considered normal, then the following would most likely
happen.

The police would realize from the story that this was primarily
a psychiatric problem and would attempt to get the patient
hospitalized for a psychiatric evaluation. They might call the
family physician or the family attorney who would advise them
that in the last few months serious concern was noted about the
patient's psychiatric problems. In fact, the family physician
might quite responsibly and ethically state that, on the basis of
the developing history and behavior, even with superficial
knowledge of psychiatry a certain number of differential
diagnoses could be considered as being responsible for the
behavior in question. One of these could be the development of
cancer in the brain. The second possibility is the acute onset of a
manic-depressive psychosis which occurs in this age group and
which manifests itself with grandiose social and psychological
behavior. The other possibility might be the flowering of some
long-standing neurotic pathology and repressed hostility towrds
the wife, and finally (and least likely nowadays), would be
syphilis of the central nervous system, which is not as common as
it was in the past, but which still occurs even among the upper

classes and is known as "general paralysis of the insane" (GPI). Now, in addition, any variety of other psychogenic or organic illnesses could cause the onset of such symptomatology.

There can be no question that a brain tumor is a strictly organic, pathological disease entity which can be documented by radiological and other laboratory findings. Furthermore, there is little question that it is primarily a specific disease entity as organic as a tumor of the breast. However, while tumors in the lungs manifest themselves by coughing and shortness of breath, the initial symptoms of many brain tumors tend to be psychological. The cases described above illustrate problems of quite clear-cut and imminent physical danger to the patient as well as raise serious diagnostic problems for the physician. In most of these situations, there is at least a distinct possibility that organic factors may be influencing the behavior as well as the psychological state of the individual. Intellectual honesty demands, however, the admission that such cases tend to be comparatively rare and that, in psychiatry as well as in the rest of medical practice, problems tend to be in the borderline area where diagnoses are not clear and treatments are often empirical. Medical students and the laity which, in this case, includes the legal profession, continually forget that the majority of diagnoses are only established over a period of time and that the likelihood of making a definitive as well as a correct diagnosis on the first contact with the patient is very rare indeed. Most cases, whether they be of physical or of mental problems, require observation over a period of time in addition to the clinical and scientific skills of the practitioner. More often than not, they require various therapeutic trials of treatment before the optimum treatment is established and occasionally before the diagnostic entity and the etiology of the problem are discovered.

A case comes to mind which raises problems in psychiatric intervention. Recently, a resident contacted me and described a case in which the following were the essential factors. A woman in her thirties with a ten-year history of various psychiatric state hospital admissions came on her own accord to the emergency room of the University hospital, complaining of pain all over her body which she attributed to physical abuse by parties unknown!

Examination revealed scattered and multiple recent bruises but no serious or permanent damage. The history as to the exact way that she received these bruises tended to be vague. The patient was discharged from the emergency room and, in retrospect, we discovered that she wandered off on her own to the psychiatric inpatient unit where she walked in and started writing on the blackboard. The psychiatric resident was alerted to this and came to chat with the patient who, it has to be emphasized, had already been discharged from the emergency room. A complicated and rather vague discussion took place between the resident and the patient in which the resident most likely made a correct diagnosis of an acute schizophrenic process manifested by certain delusions, poor judgment, disordered content of thought and inappropriate affect. The patient who had wandered into the inpatient unit proceeded to threaten the resident with all kinds of bodily harm should he take any steps to hospitalize her in the unit. Having had a previous record of institutional commitment, she also threatened to kill him should she be committed. The resident consulted me by telephone and stated that, in his opinion, this woman was quite sick, suffering from a severe schizophrenic exacerbation, that in her own way she was looking for help and that her coming to the inpatient unit was a form of a cry for help. He had the good sense to call the emergency room and from there establish her address and the telephone numbers of her relatives and contacted them prior to calling me.

The relatives all expressed an opinion that the patient was very sick and that, hopefully, the doctor would be able to hospitalize her, since admissions to hospitals seemed always to improve the patient even if the improvement were temporary and, obviously, related to medicine intake and compliance. The resident was quite disturbed with my judgment that an emergency commitment should not be initiated. In all fairness, I think this was a borderline decision which, with merit, could go both ways. I advised the resident more on the basis of my concern with legal statutes rather than medical welfare. The resident felt that the patient, in her own psychotic manner, was looking for help and that it was his obligation as a physician to do everything he could to help her. He was concerned that once she left the hospital she might again get herself involved in some altercation in which she could get hurt or possibly hurt somebody else. There is no question that his concern was legitimate. My advice was based on the fact that this patient did not present an imminent physical threat to anyone or to herself, that this was mere speculation, however well-grounded in theory, and that this was the kind of situation in which, according to the letter of the law, a probate commitment should be undertaken rather than an emergency physician's certificate. I told the resident to advise the relatives that if they continued to be concerned they should take the matter to the local probate court.

However, in my experience, the majority of psychiatrists would, in all likelihood, commit the patient, particularly after reviewing the previous history and the family's inclination expressed on the telephone. Furthermore, in the majority of cases, antipsychotic drugs would probably make a distinct improvement in the patient's condition. From a legal perspective, my advice was probably correct; from a medical point of view and the patient's medical interests, the most expeditious way of procuring help for the patient would have been to follow the resident's wishes. In fact, the patient was shortchanged by the statutes of Connecticut. (24)

It is perhaps this gray area in which psychiatry is confronted by social, human and psychological dilemmas that presents the greatest degree of problem, concern and inchoate thinking. It is in this area and in problems stemming from such cases that the criticism of psychiatry has erupted. This case can be contrasted with an event that occurred at the University Health Center recently enough for it to be also well imprinted in my mind and memory. Acting as back-up to a psychiatric nurse, I was involved in a situation as follows: A young black male wandered onto the inpatient unit, having been steered that way from the emergency room of the hospital. He looked perplexed, confused, and at times appeared to smile in a rather inappropriate manner and generally displayed behavior which gave the nurse a feeling that he was "flaky." He was unable to answer questions as to his age and address and unable to respond as to what he wanted from the staff. At times he would stand up, smiling somewhat inappropriately but conveying a feeling of a certain embarrassment as well as of a wish not to embarrass or intrude on other people's time and efforts. He would make a halfhearted effort to walk away, but after two or three paces without any intervention from anyone around him, would stop, look bewildered, turn around and come back. Occasionally, one could see an effort made on his part to verbalize, but the words were so soft-spoken that they were quite unintelligible. Since the patient had wandered in by himself and there was nobody available to give any history or information, I decided to treat him as some acute case of amnesia and had him walked back to the emergency room with a request that a comprehensive physical examination be done to rule out any possibility of acute injury as well as requesting that the emergency room staff go through this young man's pockets to find if there were any identification.

Both of these steps were performed. The physical examination revealed no injury or any other physical illness, which is what I suspected clinically, and the search of the young man's pockets, performed with one of the security officers present, found a wallet, identification card and address. The relatives were traced quite quickly, and the young man's mother arrived. She gave the history that approximately five weeks prior to this he had been hospitalized for one week at a local community hospital in its Psychiatry Department, was uncooperative, did not go along with the treatments recommended and was discharged without any follow-up being implemented by their clinic. The only advice that was given was to find a private psychiatrist which, for this black family, was quite unrealistic and impossible.

The mother was quite concerned about her son — her oldest — stated that he had lost his father in a car accident five years before, had recently begun to be depressed and to talk about joining his father and feeling guilt at being alive while his father was dead. His initial hospitalization (voluntary, informal) was precipitated by periods of wandering around at night in the streets, depression, lack of concentration, difficulty with appetite, and the inability to understand what was going on around him. There were a number of arrests at night, since his behavior on the streets, probably similar to what was observed by us on the unit and the emergency room, would most obviously attract attention as somewhat peculiar and potentially suspicious. His inability to respond to the police officer's questions would, at times, elicit some verbal abuse and a number of arrests which were not pursued after the family had been contacted. Most recently, the precipitant for this last episode appeared to relate to the issue of the young man's having been told by his girl friend that she was going to have his baby and his friends' telling him that he was a fool to believe her. The mother was most insistent in wanting help for her son.

The following brief clinical vignettes describe the variety of problems that present to the emergency room or confront the psychiatrist. In each of these situations I was, in some way, consulted as attending faculty by a resident who felt troubled by the problem. In all three cases, my advice was made on the basis of a mixture of concern for the patient's welfare as well as with an eye on the statutes. Or, as I advise the residents, "Do what is in the patient's best interests, but do not transgress his legal rights!"

On a week-end night the psychiatric resident described a problem on the medical inpatient unit. He had been called to see a forty-five-year-old man with a long-standing history of alcoholism who was in need of medication to control both a seizure activity (epilepsy) as well as very high blood pressure which was potentially life-threatening. The psychiatrist was called because the patient had behaved bizarrely on the inpatient unit, refusing to take medicines, asking the nurse to leave the medicines in his room and to walk out so that he could take it in his own privacy, and the assumption was that he was not complying. The patient would get dressed and make half-hearted gestures of walking out. The medical resident responsible for the treatment of this patient, overworked and frustrated by this uncooperative patient, decided that this was a clear-cut case of psychotic behavior and that psychiatry should accept responsibility for the patient.

The psychiatric resident was particularly concerned about the possibility of intellectual impairment; that is, organic damage due to the long history of alcoholic abuse, but could not document anything which would not be within normal and acceptable limits for a man of that particular socioeconomic and educational background. In fact, he stated that, apart from the possibility that this patient was somewhat suspicious and unreasonable and because of his huge size physically scared the nurses, there was really nothing else that he could document.

The medical resident responded by saying that the psychiatric resident should make a judgment that this man was "incompetent" so that they could then proceed to force medicines by injection if necessary.

The psychiatric resident had enough background in legal psychiatry to know that it takes more than a physician to make such a judgment, but still felt sympathetic to the plight of his medical colleague and called me for help. After hearing the story, my only piece of advice was one that obviously was most unhelpful. I stated that, actually, grounds for commitment did not exist, and since the patient was being coerced psychologically into taking his medicines, there was a possibility that one could argue that his informed consent was being abused. I advised that the patient be confronted and told forthwith that he either remove himself from the hospital if he was dissatisfied with the treatment and the disposition of the physicians or that he go along with the regulations which were there to entail and guarantee his best treatment and his welfare. The medical resident was so incensed at this "inhuman" advice that he told the psychiatric resident to tell this to the patient himself, which the psychiatric resident proceeded to do. A follow-up of this case showed that the patient from that time on began to participate and cooperate actively in his treatment. He might just as well have walked out, and medicine would have once again been angry at psychiatry's unreasonableness. However, no other medical management seemed reasonable.

Again, on a different evening — and these problems inevitably occur on week-ends and at night — a husband dropped off his wife at the emergency room following a suicidal attempt. She was obviously drunk; the husband, who was also inebriated, said that this was her third suicidal attempt in the last two years, that she had been committed before and that she'd been talking about suicide the last few days. The suicide was by ingestion of some tranquilizing medication, and the facts were somewhat vague.

Her stomach was pumped out, but the patient was obviously still quite sedated, though in no physical danger. The husband, at this point, had disappeared. There was no telephone number left. The resident felt that he was left holding the problem and wondered what he should do. I suggested that the patient be allowed to sleep overnight in the hospital even though she had not signed herself in and even though she had not made an informed consent judgment for her hospitalization. My advice was based on the fact that I predicted the patient on waking up would probably either be well enough to go home or sign in for further stay. In the actual event, the second happened. However, this was an "indigent" case, and one wonders what would have happened if this patient had been billed for an overnight stay. I doubt whether the hospital could have successfully or easily been reimbursed.

To conclude, let me describe two situations with two different resolutions, both tragic from the point of view of the individuals concerned. A female patient in her 30's was brought to the emergency room by the police and a visiting public health nurse. The story was that the patient had not been paying her bills, that complaints had been launched against her, and, since she had not paid her rent, the landlord decided that she ought to be evicted. Someone had enough information to raise the issue of psychiatric problem, and the police took a public health nurse with them on a house visit. The nurse found her a withdrawn, shy woman who seemed to be unable to comprehend the concern caused by her actions and who had in her possession a number of welfare checks that had not been cashed. The patient was brought to the emergency room by the police and easily persuaded to sign herself in voluntarily for treatment. Did she really understand what she had signed, and was she capable of understanding? Should she have been given the benefit of being put in jail as a debtor? Should she have been evicted from her apartment on the grounds that she was exercising rational judgment? Had the psychiatrists abused her freedom and coerced her?

A similar case concerned a married couple who continually felt that neighbors were persecuting them by driving by and emitting various kinds of smells and other nuisances. The couple continually called the police, who responded no less than approximately 100 times in less than six months. A public health nurse was involved again in this situation and could make no sense out of the tragedy. She asked for a psychiatric consultation to which the couple agreed and which I conducted. They were cooperative, friendly, stated that they realized that the story sounded improbable and crazy but that, indeed, it was true. There were no psychiatric symptoms that I could elicit; they did not wish any treatment; they wanted to be able to live in their house, to continue working — which they were doing — and not to be bothered by the nuisances performed by their jealous neighbors. The dismay of the public health nurse was overwhelming when I informed her that there was nothing that I could advise or suggest. Sooner or later, however, in this situation either the symptoms of paranoia will increase and some tragedy will occur or the police officers will lose their cool and begin to harrass the couple.

Having developed the medical tradition for the confinement and involuntary treatment of the mentally ill and having described a variety of problems that psychiatrists are forced to confront not because of their megalomanic wish for empire building but because they are the ones to whom society turns for help, I am forced to comment that the guidelines for such intervention are extremely scanty. The statutes have been written by attorneys, usually in response to either legal or social pressure. They are varied in scope and will be discussed at length in Chapter VI. However, New York State has progressive and protective laws. (25)

One of the best medical comments on this whole situation comes from a lecture by Dr. Charles A. Mercier who, in 1906, wrote that, "Anyone who from mental unsoundness is unable to manage his affairs in any department, may legally and properly be detainable." He goes on to qualify this by stating that, "What is legal, is not always expedient, and it is not expedient in every case to do what is legally permissible." He then notes the following indication for considering the expediency of committment: mental illness leading to the need for protection for others and of himself or herself. Dr. Mercier emphasizes that what is inevitably missing in statutory language and the cause of much acrimony (this in 1906) is the overriding factor that, "There is another reason equally important to either of them, and that is in order that the person may receive skilled treatment with a view to his recovery." (26)

In his excellent book, Kittire argues that Judge Shaw, in the 1845 ruling in the famous case of Mr. Josiah Oaks opened up the gates of the therapeutic state. (27)

While Professor Kittrie sees this as the beginning of the current problem, it may also be seen as a juridical reflection that there are certain inherent rights that the community owes its individual citizen. These include the rights of happiness and of privacy, the right to freedom and liberty and to be considered innocent until proven guilty. But in a day and age in which medical treatment as such is no longer considered to be a privilege but a right, when education is no longer considered to be a privilege of the upper classes but also a duty owed every child, then it is reasonable to assume that the right to medical treatment and treatment from disease is inherent in the community. Is it so unreasonable to assume that the right to medical treatment and to be free from disease is such a revolutionary and novel idea?

Certainly in the 1970's, as we are confronted with arguments about the skyrocketing costs of medical care which make illness a catastrophic experience for some families, as we argue the social justice of providing for the elderly as well as of providing basic medical care for those who are unable to take care of themselves, it does not seem so unreasonable to consider that freedom from all diseases and disorders and a right to treatment is an inherent right of the citizen. The issue of the medical model and mental disorder is a legitimate question and will be discussed in Chapter III. However, if given that premise, then the expectation that treatment is obligatory and an inherent right of the citizen seems logically well established.

It has now been argued by some psychiatrists that the provision of psychiatric services falls into a sphere which is not medical but which has to do with human resources, such as public and free education, welfare support of the indigent, workman's compensations, permanent disability insurance and special assistance to the handicapped. These arguments have been advanced quite strongly and with considerable merit, and there is no question that many aspects of mental health services and of those aspects of treatment which have to do with the custodial care aspect fall in line with humanitarian services better than with medical. Yet, again, there is little question that in acute situations the most appropriate model for intervention is the medical one. If, indeed, psychiatry thinks that the medical tradition for the intervention in the mentally disordered is worth preserving, that it is in the best interests of society and of prospective patients and that, indeed, it is within the province and competence of the medical profession and its sub-specialty psychiatry, then some of the criticisms that have been directed towards it have to be faced, and some of the looseness of thinking has to be tightened.

NOTES

1. H. E. Sigerist, "What medicine has contributed to the progress of civilization," *International Record of Medicine and General Practice Clinics, 168:*383-391 (1955).

2. B. N. Braginsky, and D. T. Braginsky, "Mental hospitals as resorts," *Psychology Today,* March (1973).

3. Group for the Advancement of Psychiatry, Memo. #4, Commitment Procedures 1948. It is interesting to compare this with the second report in 1966: *Laws governing hospitalization of the mentally ill.* Address: Group for the Advancement of Psychiatry, 104 E. 25th Street, New York City.

4. J. B. Robitscher,"Psycho-surgery and other somatic means of altering behavior," *Bulletin of the American Academy of Psychiatry and the Law,* 2:7-33 (1974). A discussion of some of the polemics: V. Snodgrass, "Debate of the benefits and ethics of psychosurgery involves public," *Journal of American Medicine,* 225:913-920 (1973). Also look at Dr. Vernon Mark's interesting letter reported in *Journal of American Psychiatry,* 227:943 (February, 1974).

5. Solomon, Hirsch, "Observations of the Identity Problems of Psychiatrists." Paper read at the 1972 meeting of Canadian Psychiatric Association. In this paper the author analyzes the far-reaching positions taken in official presidential addresses of the American Psychiatric Association between 1961 and 1969. Dr. Hirsch documents that in these years there was a growing tendency for psychiatry to become involved in social action that would influence mankind.

Dr. Hirsch quotes a selection of these addresses: "There will be applications far beyond your offices and your hospital... application to the human relations of normal people in politics, national and international, between races, between capital and labour, in government... in every form of human relationship — you will be concerned with optimum performances of human beings as civilized creatures." "Actually no less than the entire world is a proper catchment area for present day psychiatry." "We have available theory and experience to guide those in decision-making positions."

6. L. Bellak, "The Need for Public Health Laws for Psychiatric Illness," *American Journal of Public Health*, 61:119-121 (1971).

7. *New York Times*, May 5th, 1968, p. 62.

8. S. L. Halleck, *The Politics of Therapy* (New York, Science House, 1971).

9. Recently I was asked to see a surgical patient in consultation whose main problem was that she was "cheating" on her diet. The surgeon asked me to intervene and also outlined a complex plan for monitoring her visitors and all ward contacts who could in any way be responsible for smuggling food to her on the ward. After hearing the story, I suggested that the surgeon tell the patient that her abuse of the prescribed diet was incompatible with treatment and that if she (the patient) thought so little of the doctor's efforts, the outcome of her treatment or her own life, then certainly there was no point in wasting all this effort and staff time. The surgeon listened to my remarks with incredulity and replied that he was a physician and had to save the patient's life and health.

10. DSM-11. Diagnostic and Statistical Manual of Mental Disorders. Second edition. Committee on Nomenclature & Statistics of the A.P.A. Published A.P.A. 1700 18th Street, N.W., Washington, D.C. 20009. 1968. Also see ft 4, Chapter I.

11. Leach V. Overholser, 257 F. 2d 667 (D.C. Cir. 1957). Discussed in J. Katz, J. Goldstein, and A. M. Dershowitz, *Psychoanalysis, Psychiatry and Law* (New York, New York Free Press, 1967), pp. 602-614.

12. D. L. Bazelon, "Psychiatrists and the adversary process," *Scientific American*, 230:18-23 (1974).

13. An excellent review of some of the problems pertaining to our environmental versus genetic perception of behavior with comprehensive review of literature can be found in D. Freeman, "Aggression: Instinct of symptom," *Australian and New Zealand Journal of Psychiatry*, 5:66-77 (1971).

14. E. Freidson *Professional Dominance* (New York, Atherton Press, 1970).

15. M. Roth, "Psychiatry and its critics," *Canadian Psychiatric Journal*, 17:343-350. this was a presidential address to the Royal College of Psychiatrists by Sir Martin Roth. Also, L. Eisenberg, "The Future of Psychiatry," *Lancet*, 1371-1375 (1973).

16. F. L. Bartlett, "Present Day Requirements for State Hospitals Joining the Community," *New England Journal of Medicine*, 276:90-94 (1967). But while the problem of the non-English-speaking psychiatrist is obvious and well-documented, some further objective facts of this problem need to be mentioned.

The foreign-trained medical graduate (FMG) tends to gravitate into paid salaried positions. The best analysis of the current situation is contained in the book *Foreign Trained Physicians in American Medicine*, by Rosemary Stevens and JoAn Vermeulan, Division of Manpower Intelligence, Bureau of Health Manpower Intelligence, N.I.H., 1972. This study documented certain interesting facts. At the end of December, 1970, there were a total of 57,217 FMG in the United States, which made up 17.1 percent of all physicians in the United Staes at that time. As many as 10,563 were involved in full-time salaried hospital-based practice, making up 30.3 percent of those positions. For psychiatric practice the following statistics are significant: there are 5,025 FMG in psychiatry, 1,891 (23.8% of the FMG psychiatrists) in full-time staff positions (which is 40.5% of all these positions).

While the obvious weaknesses and the comparatively poor training of the majority of FMGs is only too readily noted in literature, the following usually escapes attention: that 1,006 are in full-time medical school teaching (18% of all such positions) and 3,285 are in full-time research (27.5% of all such positions) and that for psychiatry specifically, 216 are in teaching and research, which is 20 percent of the total figure. The point here is that while the spectrum of expertise may very well be greater than for American graduates, as a matter of record foreign medical graduates in this country have both enjoyed the opportunity of participating in academic and research work and have been considered productive enough to be employed in such capacities and compare favorably with American medical school graduates.

17. Major psychiatric textbooks have provided few guidelines to assist psychiatrists in determining appropriate criteria for involuntary hospitalization. In one major textbook, Dr. J. Katz writes:

> Interestingly, however, the behavioral sciences have not yet been able to evolve simple and operational definitions of eccentricity or of dangerousness. As therapeutic interventions increase in intensity and scope, they more frequently encounter the question of a person impulsively leaving treatment where there appears to be a good chance that he could further improve his status and diminish his self-destructive behavior. Without some element of restraint, such a person might not have received therapeutic help at all. Nonetheless, it is probably best, both for society and for therapy of the patient, that

coercion be restricted to the minimum necessary for the protection of life.

J. Katz, "Law and Psychiatry," in F. Redlich, and D. X. Friedman, *Theory and Practice of Psychiatry* (New York, Basic Books, 1966). In his chapter on forensic psychiatry in the *Comprehensive Textbook of Psychiatry*, one of the most widely used texts in the United States, Dr. Lawrence Z. Friedman writes,

> In fact, however, for the lawyer a commitment is a mittimus, a warrant for imprisonment. On the other hand, for the psychiatrist the term denotes a helpful procedure, in that it facilitates the hospitalization and appropriate treatment of a patient as mentally ill.

L. Z. Friedman, "Forensic Psychiatry," in A. M. Freedman, and H. T. Kaplan, eds., *Comprehensive Textbook of Psychiatry* (Baltimore, Williams and Wilkins, 1967). In another well-known text Dr. Henry Davidson (H. A. Davidson, "The commitment procedures and their legal implications," in S. Arieti, ed., *American Handbook of Psychiatry* (New York, Basic Books, 1959), a well-known forensic psychiatrist, in a chapter entitled "The Commitment Procedures and Their Legal Implications" describes the variety and confused aspect of state requirements for commitments. He gives some general warnings to physicians and psychiatrists on the steps to be followed, but does not in any way address himself to the indications of emergency commitment. The nearest that is stated is that "A physician that cannot demonstrate to a judge that the patient is psychotic has a weak case." This point is made in context of testifying before a judge to the advisability of a probate commitment, usually a step which follows or which would normally have followed an emergency intervention. In the section on hospitalization of the mentally ill in Detre and Jarecki's *Modern Psychiatric Treatment* (Philadelphia, Lippincott & Company, 1971), there is nothing whatsoever about involuntary commitment and the words "commitment," "certification," and "involuntary" do not even appear in the index.

18. J. B. Robitscher, supra footnote 4 and "The Right to Psychiatric Treatment: A Social Approach to the Plight of the State Hospital Patient," *Villanova Law Journal*, 18:11-36 (1972). A question of the kind of treatment was taken to the Supreme Court of New York, and it was ruled that shock treatment could not necessarily be given to an involuntarily hospitalized patient if that patient refused to consent to its administration. This rather paradoxical finding in that a patient could refuse appropriate treatment for her or his illness and yet be involuntarily confined for his welfare can only be explained by the current climate of doubt as to the efficacy of electric-convulsive therapy and the general fear of manipulating the brain in any physical manner. The judge ruled that in view of the fact that there was some question as to the indication for this treatment the patient should be given "the benefit" of the doubt and not subjected to this specific treatment. *New York Law Journal* (July, 1972).

19. It is really difficult to establish the philosophy that is behind the majority of statutes pertaining to the emergency commitment of the mentally ill. It would seem reasonable and has been so ruled by Judge Blumenfeld in Connecticut (Logan v. Arafeh-316 F. Supp. 1265, 1972) that the criteria for such emergency commitment should be limited to danger to self and others as a result of mental illness, this danger being defined as physical danger. In that same ruling, pertaining to a Connecticut suit, the same judge stated that the criteria for probate commitment could be more general and broader so as to enable sick people to get treatment. This is a common sense decision. In a troublesome acute case, only the most heroic measures should be undertaken, but when benefits of treatment versus nontreatment are considered, then it makes sense to bring psychological, social factors into the decision-making process. On the other hand, in that same ruling, the judge supported the Connecticut statutes which allowed the emergency commitment to be extended to a forty-five-day period and argued the benefits of this as being necessary to give emergency treatment the best scope for success.

The language for the emergency and probate commitment tends to be archaic. Certainly when treatment in psychiatry was nothing better than custodial care, then one could argue the benefits of incarceration only for prevention of dangerousness. Given the current situation in which progressively more complex, complicated and hence potentially dangerous as well as effective treatments are available, it is difficult to decide at what point such treatment is covered by these statutes and at which point it should be omitted pending a probate court's adjudication of the need for further involuntary treatment or of competency to decide the issue of informed consent.

In the *Logan v. Arafeh* decision, the judge stated that the period of time should be extensive enough so that treatment would begin to be effective and thus probate commitments would be lessened. It would seem expedient from one point of view; on the other hand, one could argue that the court, if confronted by a case that was still in its active psychotic turmoil, would have an easier decision whether to commit or not and that ultimately the concern of society to protect the individual rights of its citizens would be better served by a minimum form of treatment following emergency confinement with adjudication by a court as quickly as possible.

20. In a recent law class discussion, the issue of patients' being protected from psychiatrists by attorneys was discussed. If indeed the question of informed consent and mental competence and mental illness were the reason that the person was brought to the hospital or the emergency room in the first place, it made no sense to have the patient protected from the psychiatrist by an attorney — my argument being that an attorney would not be in a position to extract informed consent, if indeed the patient was sick. I elaborated this point one step further by suggesting that, indeed, there was no evidence that society wished to have the attorney get involved, that society really wished for legal intervention

when members of their families or they themselves might be sick. This suggestion elicited a discussion with one rather interesting comment which I think is very much a reflection of the attorneys' perception of their own role. A law student stated that essentially the medical profession, in the exercise of their duties, were given those privileges by and controlled by law and, therefore, it was up to *the law to determine how it was practiced.* My comment, in turn, was that the mandate to practice medicine antedates the legal system, the constitution and written law, and is mandated to the medical profession by society and administered by laws made by society through legislatures. Regardless of the aspects of this argument, the fact remains that a number of attorneys do feel that they are the sole and only protectors of "freedom" of society — an argument which is particularly difficult to accept in the aftermath of Watergate.

21. It has been paradoxical that many attorneys who take a very jaundiced view of psychiatric interventions argue wholeheartedly the merits of decriminalizing alcoholism. Yet, the potential for coercion to get alcoholics to undergo detoxifying treatment is far more obvious.

22. S. L. Halleck, "Legal and Ethical Aspects of Behavior Control," *American Journal of Psychiatry*, 131:381-385 (1974).

23. The problems inherent in this are discussed by the Devil's Advocate: *Bulletin of the American Academy of Psychiatry and Law*, 2:64-65 (1974) and by R. Slovenko, *Psychiatry and Law* (Boston, Little, 1973) (particularly Chapter XIV — "Rights of Committed Patients') and again J. G. Robitscher, see supra fn 4, and D. Wexler, *Cases and Materials in Prison inmate legal assistance*, Washington, D.C., U..S. Government Printing Office, 1974.

24. Connecticut General Statutes, Rev. 17-184 and 17-178, 1971, speak to the fact that the physician has to state, "I am of the opinion that the above named person is in immediate need of care and treatment in a hospital for mental illness because his or her mental condition presents a danger to himself or others."

25. New York State Mental Hygiene Law, Amended 1973 — Article 31. The undersigned physician has to certify the following points: 1. That he is a physician licensed to practice medicine in New York State. 2. That he has shown care and diligence in a personal observation and examination of the patient. 3. That he finds that this individual has a mental illness which requires care and treatment as an inpatient for that individual's welfare and, furthermore, that there is such impairment of judgment that patient himself is unable to understand need for such care and treatment. The physician, furthermore, has to state that he has considred alternative forms of care and treatment, but that in his judgment they are inadequate to provide for the needs of the patient or are not readily avialable. The patient's welfare is, furthermore, reasonably well protected by the New York Mental Health Information Service which in two of

the districts of New York State is staffed by attorneys and in two by social workers, a rather paradoxical situation. For an excellent review of the functioning of this agency, see R. K. Gupta, "New York's Mental Health Information Service: An experiment in due process," *Rutgers Law Review*, 25:405-450 (1971).

26. C. A. Mercier, "A lecture on Certifiability," *The Clinical Journal*, 29:280-286 (1906;1907).

27. N. N. Kittrie, *The Right to be Different* (Baltimore, Johns Hopkins, 1972).

CHAPTER III

THE CONCEPT OF MENTAL ILLNESS

THE whole premise underlying the concept of involuntary hospitalization is currently based on one of (or a combination of) the following postulates: that the individual in question is mentally ill and dangerous or that the patient is mentally ill and in need of treatment for his own welfare, a state which he does not recognize because of the *severity* of his mental illness.

The problem in both cases is the concept of the disease model as a causal (not pragmatic) explanation for mental illness. If, indeed, mental illness does not exist, if it is nothing else but a construct to explain a form of behavior that the rest of society finds alien and obnoxious and if it does *not* intrude on the free will or decision-making aspect of the individual, then commitment should not take place, and the whole practice should be abolished forthwith!

Our Anglo-Saxon tradition prohibits the concept of preventive detention. A citizen has either committed an act that is criminal and may be arrested, is in the process of committing an injurious act and may be legitimately stopped or restrained or is possibly planning or thinking about it and *cannot* be apprehended.

If mental illness does not exist, if it is merely a psychosocial cultural expression of inability to cope with a difficult or impossible situation (as in my judgment are all forms of neurotic or hysterical reaction), then involuntary hospitalization can under no circumstance be justified. A detention or apprehension for some time may be in order and both legal and ethical as, for example, preventing an individual who threatens to jump off a bridge from actually jumping. A "cooling off" period may be helpful, but treatment cannot be enforced because there is no illness.

If there is no such disease entity, then it makes no sense to agonize over commitment statutes or laws, making them restrictive or otherwise, since it is an exercise in futility and furthermore, a dishonest compromise between old medical tradition and new scientific reality!

Some critics of the commitment process argue that involuntary hospitalization is detention without due process, to prevent an occurrence of an act which is unlikely to happen!

If there is no mental illness, then involuntary hospitalization for mental illness and dangerousness is indeed exactly what the critics would say — prevention and unreasonable detention without due process.

But if mental illness does not exist, then society and the legal process have been fooled and have fooled themselves for thousands of years, and concepts such as insanity and incompetency also have to be abolished.

It is certainly true that for a theoretical postulate an argument can be made and sustained that mental impairment (for example, due to senility or brain damage due to accident) may exist without either validating or rejecting the concept of mental illness. "Abolishing" mental illness does not need to mean that the law has to treat a brain-injured citizen as possessing full mental competency or accept the obviously inequitable fact that all do have testamentary capacity.

Furthermore, I am quite prepared to accept the possibility that social behavior due to social stress may be considered as exculpating in criminal accountability or as precipitating a state of maladaptive behavior.

Our society, in the United States in particular, is certainly attracted to these ideas, and hence the ambivalence as to whether psychiatric facilities and mental health clinics are inherently medical, part of the human resources agencies, or separate from all and possessing unique features which make them a separate social discipline!

To accept the truth of one does not deny truth to the other. That is, both may be right, one or the other may be right, and both may be wrong.

It is my conviction that both are operative. Individuals do react with acute catastrophic anxiety to stressful situations and do it in a way that is culturally sanctioned and acceptable for their background.

Certain "syndromes" or "idiosyncracies" are associated with particular cultural groups, and anthropologists have studied these reactions quite extensively. (1)

However, it is the intent of this chapter to argue that certain forms of emotional disorders, even so-called functional disorders are as much a disease as are multiple sclerosis and cancer!

Webster defines disease as "an unhealthy condition of the body or mind." It is a condition which lowers the sense of well-being of the individual, reduces his adaptiveness and impairs his ability to function in his given milieu or, in psychoanalytic language, "expectable environment."

Relativists have argued these points extensively and have postulated questions such as: in a country where the tsetse fly is found and sleeping sickness prevalent and yet where the association between the two is not understood and the fact of illness accepted, does that mean the "natives" are not sick? Or for that matter, is black lung of the Kentucky coal miner not a disease simply because it has been accepted as a way of life for many generations? Does the fact that the "black lung" is due to environmental situations preclude it from being a medical illness?

Prior to the understanding of the transmission of infectious illness by bacteria less than 200 years ago, was that lack of understanding a reasonable basis for denying the reality of diseases such as meningitis and the bubonic plague? Since we do not know what actually causes cancer, is it any less a disease?

In fact, we see that what is now accepted as the medical model of illness only developed in the last 200 years. In fact, it can be well argued that the general public's understanding of illness is too simplistic, that the natural course of illness is affected by many factors, some of these only now being worked out as problems of environmental stress, psychological attitudes, self-perception, character strength, and of course, to a large extent, predetermined by the inheritance of genes! (2)

The 19th century model of a "bug" assaulting a host organism resulting in infection which becomes an illness is too simplistic, in fact not accurate, and yet remains the lay person's (and this includes attorneys and social workers) understanding of the medical model.

All medicine, all of the practice of medicine, is, in fact, psychosomatic in the sense that social, psychological, and physical factors are intertwined. Those physicians who practice the layman's perception of medicine are practicing a specialized form of medicine, not the sole and only form of medicine. Those critics who state that medicine and physicians do not pay attention to environmental factors are simply ignoring a multitude of practical and theoretical concerns of the medical profession, such as developing criteria for drinking water, space in dormitories, nutritional standards, etc.

It has been accepted that disease entities are developed through the scientific study of syndromes. Not too many years ago hypertension was a syndrome which could be observed, diagnosed, and whose ill effects were well documented. We now know that for this syndrome there are many different etiologies interplaying with each other, such as build, diet, stress, and genetic inheritance.

But a disease entity can be established on the basis of observable data, a course of the disease, and outcome. Organic mental disease and functional mental disease have these attributes.

My contention is to develop the point that the concept of mental illness, both from an historical and from a current scientific validity, is as real, can be as well documented, defined, diagnosed, and treated as is pneumonia, multiple sclerosis or cancer.

But, at the same time, I have to emphatically state that the variety of personality disorders and neuroses that have in the United States fallen within the purview of psychiatry by the route of being amenable to the reeducation process of psychoanalysis are not forms of mental illness.

My contention is also as strong that not every diagnostic category or label or description of behavior or of conduct falls within the meaning and understanding of the term "mental illness." Unfortunately here we are paying the price for the overwhelming influence, if not monopoly, in American psychiatry of psychoanalytic psychology which, in a very understandable and logical way, developed a series of categories for describing certain personality traits and characteristics. These particular psychoanalytically derived descriptions of behavior have tended to become value judgments, and some at least have a mildly perjorative quality. They were standarized during the Second World War by the psychiatric profession which used them often in an administrative manner, helping the armed forces of the United States in separations of unwanted individuals from active service. (3) Therefore, it is not surprising that there are labels such as anxiety neuroses or inadequate personality together with diagnostic criteria which have a scientific validity such as arteriosclerotic brain disease or schizophrenia.

We fail to find personality labels such as "hard-working," "striving" or such descriptions as "competitive" and "successful." People with such personalities, if they come to the attention of psychiatrists, are perceived as having positive ego strengths! Even the vague possibility that some individuals may be involuntarily hospitalized for neurotic problems is particularly troublesome to those intelligent and thinking people in the community who have themselves experienced neurotic anxieties and depressions, who have coped and perhaps, in some way, been strengthened by the experience of their ordeal. Furthermore, there are irrefutable arguments that some forms of neurotic conflict have creative and positive values as documented in the life histories of many famous writers, composers and men of science.

Furthermore, an unfortunate analogy is often developed from the analytic treatment context. For successful analysis to be undertaken, the individual has to have a basic inherent motivation for change. While all of us recognize that there may be certain coercions of psychic anxiety or even external coercions in the realization that certain patterns of behavior are maladaptive to professional or interpersonal success, yet it is the individual who decides that he has certain personality or intrapsychic liabilities, and it is the individual who makes a decision and a judgment in which direction he pursues his personality development. The patient prescribes his "treatment," the patient outlines his goals and the limits of personality change that are compatible with his self-image and amount of discomfort.

For a society like America in which "psychological" thinking permeates the educational system, in which psychoanalytically derived concepts are used to explain and too often to excuse all kinds of problems, from social ineptitude to crime, in which each and all of us are made aware that we have unconscious conflicts, identity problems and "hang-ups," psychiatry has a prestige, is endowed with influence and, to some extent, steps into the shoes of moral philosophy as a guiding authority. Since it has none of these attributes and since it lets the hopeful down, it is perceived in an ambivalent fashion at best and negatively by those looking for a meaning in their lives.

Many of us, if not all of us, have our own little quirks of behavior which are not quite acceptable to the morals of society. Some of us enjoy sex in a way that society frowns upon (fetishism, voyeurism), while some of us do not enjoy sex as much as society implies that we should, were we really free of neurotic conflicts!

Unfortunately, these are too often and too readily identified by the psychiatric profession and psychology as forms of mental and/or emotional illness. Some appear to be passive, not aggressive. (4)

The thought, even theoretical, that someone may decide to forcefully modify our behavior, to eradicate our erotic fantasies or to make us conform to some standard of moral or ethical conduct is repugnant.

During my college days I well remember the facetious but troubling rumor that the army would use saltpeter to inhibit the sexual drive of the army conscripts!

Paranoia is endemic, but the technological opportunities for social control increase, so that what thirty years ago was a student joke and mild concern is now written up in responsible journals as a possibility to be guarded against!

To argue, therefore, that involuntary hospitalization for mental illness is an acceptable fact, it is imperative to not only prove that mental illness is a disease, but also to make sure that all these various forms of life style are *not included* in the concept!

There are however certain categories which are clearly

diagnosable and which, without treatment, have a definite natural course. Let me develop the argument from the medical model and apply it to the concept of those forms of mental illness which are organically based such as arteriosclerotic brain disease, those which are influenced by transient and toxic states such as alcoholism and those for which, currently, there is no clearly defined organic causation and which are exclusively diagnosed by observation of psychological symptoms.

In my argument I have to prove one more fact. It is not enough to substantiate the existance of mental illness, but to develop the point that mental illness is different in that it affects the decision-making process of the organism, it affects his mind, disturbs his intellectual ability such as memory, concentration, abstract thinking and judgment, disturbs the process of logical thought, impairs verbal communication, affects the symbolic processes and alienates the victim from his environment and from himself.

This is what psychiatrists call psychosis, a state of break with reality. Relativists will argue that this is a value-laden term, that can be misused. It may be misused, like everything, but:

For most of us a telephone is an electronic gadget. For the elderly it is a way of keeping in touch with friends, for the adolescent it is a gadget which brings good or bad news, for the infant it is a black (or white, etc.) object to pick up and play with, while for the tired family doctor it is a hated intrusion into his after-dinner nap. For all these people the gadget represents something tangible, different but understandable in the context of their cultural and educational experience. For the psychotic, the telephone is the "devil," it is responsible for rain, it gives off offensive smells, it controls thoughts, it affects his sexual life and it works on behalf of his mother in observing his life! That is what psychiatrists mean by psychosis: a break with reality which is incompatible with the individual's educational and cultural background.

Furthermore, as an illness it affects and inhibits the process of good judgment; it is an illness of the mind and thus impairs its function. Depending on the severity of the illness, the functioning of the individual, his very autonomy is impaired.

As people have kidney disease and this leads to the

malfunctioning of the kidney, necessitating diets, dialysis and at times resulting in death, so does mental disease follow the same rules of affecting in various ways and in different severities the functioning of the mind! Let me develop the argument from circumstances which probably will cause few disagreements.

There are a variety of organic causations of mental illness, a common one being accident-induced trauma to the brain. A concussion leads to a temporary state of unconsciousness which may occasionally be followed by severe periods of headaches and even by psychological disruption of functioning or adaptiveness such as minor irritability, transient impairment or attention and concentration and possibly a limited period of memory loss. Severe damage to the brain more seriously impairs the psychological and intellectual abilities, depending on the location and the extent of the damage and injury. Boxers were well known in the past for the severe impairment of intellectual functioning leading to the well known "punchy" boxer character in music hall comedy. However, damage to the intellectual adaptiveness of the individual often leads to the development of the same psychological states as are manifest in the functional forms of mental disease. It is not unusual to see in those people increased levels of alientation, mistrust, a flattening of affect, at times an inability to express thoughts, as well as heightened levels of apathy, depression and anxiety. Individuals who are subject to epileptic seizures often have states in which their behavior becomes automatic or in which they indulge in activities which occur as a result of dysrhythmic brain activity. In fact, some of the most controversial as well as possibly some of the most significant work in the area of neurophysiology has to do with experiments in this area, experiments which may answer the problems of impulsivity, irritability, rage and loss of control and possibly lead to therapeutic intervention.

The brain damage can be well documented in post mortem examinations; it can be electrophysiologically documented in most instances on electroencephalograms.

But toxic states such as those due to alcohol and due to metabolic problems such as diabetic coma, also lead to disruption in the functioning of the brain and to disorganized behavior. In these instances, certain laboratory studies will also document the level of blood alcohol or blood sugar. There are no arguments here that severe states impair judgment, hence, for example, the stricture against driving automobiles while under the influence of alcohol, since significant levels of alcohol impair judgment.

The critic will respond with some justification that in all these cases there is factual evidence and objective laboratory substantiation for the damage. A history of concussion can be documented, skull X-rays may show subdural bleeding, blood work may show evidence of increased sugar or of alcohol content. The critic will rightly point out that in schizophrenia and in manic-depressive psychoses there is no such "factual" evidence. Assuming even that in the next century medicine will fail to develop specific biological or other laboratory diagnostic techniques specific for the diagnosis of schizophrenia and/or manic-depressive psychoses, the following evidence, already available, is so overwhelming that it cannot be ignored. Furthermore, it is only in the second part of the 20th century that medicine has become enamoured with and identified with laboratory techniques.

Before laboratory findings were available and before medicine had research tools such as radioactive isotopes, electro-encephalograph tracings, electrocardiogram machines and other chemical tests, physicians diagnosed forms or patterns of disease on the basis of subjective symptoms as reported by the patient and objective symptoms as evidenced to the examining physician. The most common symptom in the past and now which brings patients to physicians is pain. Patients did not come for annual checkups or because they thought they might have high blood pressure. They came because they had some kind of identifiable dysphoric subjective feelings, and that usually had to do with a subjective experience of pain. No one would deny that fact that pain exists, that it can be severe, that it may be psychologically or physiologically disabling, and that it can be so severe as to disrupt everyday functioning. Even now, in our day and age of advanced scientific medicine, we have no way of measuring or gauging the severity of pain. In fact, we still have no good criteria for differentiating the pain of advanced bone cancer (by common agreement one of the most severe and tragic because it is so hard to relieve) from the pain of the hypochondriacal malingerer who uses his complaint of pain as an excuse to avoid his responsibilities or to elicit attention and sympathy.

The physician presented with a statement from a patient that he has severe chest pain with a radiation down the left arm has enough and sufficient information available right there to make a diagnosis of potential coronary occlusion. (Coronary Thrombosis or in common parlance, a heart attack.) In fact, should a physician disregard such a subjective report and sent the patient out of his office or out of the emergency room, he does so at his peril and probably risks a suit for negligence — and rightly so. Granted that currently electrocardiogram and blood studies will facilitate the diagnosis, but the diagnosis can and should be made on subjective data! The symptoms by themselves justify admission and observation of the patient if not of intensive therapeutic intervention. Thus, a series of diagnostic and therapeutic steps may be predicated on nothing more than the subjective presentation of the patient and the professional evaluation and judgment made on the basis of this information.

Osler, one of the greatest clinicians of this century, emphasized that the most important aspect of the diagnosis is a comprehensive "history." A medical history is based on what the patient reports to the physician in the context of appropriate and pertinent questions. Osler felt that the physical examination was by far the less important part of the diagnostic process. Many diagnoses, however, require the integration of the history and of the objective evidence. After all, when a physician listens to a patient's heart and hears a murmur, he is using his own judgment on what is considered normal or abnormal. The history of loss of breath, the objective evidence of an enlarged liver, swollen ankles and a murmur are all compiled together to assist the physician in making a diagnosis of heart failure.

The same is true for mental illness.

Critics of the process have commented that psychiatrists make findings to substantiate their decisions. In other words, the decision to commit is made, and then findings "manufactured" to justify the decision. In fact, large numbers of very sick schizophrenic patients are not hospitalized, let alone a significant number of patients who come to the psychiatrist.

The diagnosis of psychosis does not automatically mean legal insanity, nor does the treatment of psychosis automatically mean hospitalization, let alone commitment!

The specialty of psychiatry employs various psychological tests at times to assist in the diagnostic process and, in cases of doubt, particularly in acute situations in which voluntariness is questionable, family and friends will be contacted to get the most comprehensive data possible.

A criticism of psychiatry which is well made and to which I think the profession can plead guilty without necessarily feeling defensive is that the patient's welfare is usually taken as the most important consideration in making "management" decisions.

The physician confronted with a patient suffering a chest pain and radiation down the left arm may indeed suspect indigestion, but will, because of many factors such as concern about litigation and the safety of the patient, urge observation in a hospital.

Psychiatrists in doubt in similar situations also tend to commit. This is probably a mistake and should be *curtailed,* but it is not maliciousness, not an urge to build an empire or "have" patients, but a concern, however misguided, to protect the patient and themselves which causes them to do so. The practice should be decreased, but critics abuse good faith and integrity when they impute other motives to the majority of the medical profession.

Cross cultural studies have shown that the symptoms of schizophrenia are at times culturally influenced, but more important, that the basic diagnostic criteria are uniform. (5)

To these critics who claim that mental illness is not an illness because it is not biological or such, one can only respond by pointing to the overwhelming evidence of genetic factors. Yet genetic factors do not take away the importance of environmental stress, nor does environmental stress account for all cases of schizophrenia, which we call schizophrenic process. (6) Again, too often critics fall into a trap of their own scientific ignorance. Exposed to sociology and psychology courses that understandably emphasize sociological and psychological theories and findings which are important, they are unaware of work which is outside of their discipline or incompatible with their political theories!

I can only suggest that the critic who would say that the mentally ill are merely deviant but just labelled by psychiatric labels investigate a sociologist's review of this problem. (7) The British School of Psychiatry, which has shown greater talent and has better opportunities of epidemiological research, has also documented that schizophrenics are not just the poor and unprivileged of society, but "drift" into that position by reason of their illness. (8) Their parents represent proportionately all the socioeconomic groups prevalent in society.

The most effective form of treatment and of preventing remissions in schizophrenia is the new antipsychotic drugs and, for manics, lithium. Psychotherapy by itself is ineffective, though a useful adjunct. (9) The greatest relapse is associated with the termination of these medications. The dosages of these medicines for psychotic patients are such that normal individuals would be unable to tolerate them.

For all these reasons the genetic biological attributes of the disease process, the fact that it can be diagnosed on objective and subjective grounds and that it can be treated most effectively through biological means proves mental illness to be a disease entity.

It is a disease which impairs the individual's welfare by affecting that very organ which is so precious to all of us — our mind!

To conclude, I would emphasize that mental illness is a regression from a previously established optimum psychosocial adaptiveness. I am not referring here to the "cosmetic" psychological treatments which attempt to modify behavior, but I am referring to cases in which the psychiatrist establishes a diagnosis, prescribes treatment, and brings the patient *back* to his previous state.

I have taken pains to dissociate mental illness and involuntary hospitalization for the patient's welfare from other forms of social maladaptiveness. I do not feel that the others should necessarily *not* be treated or "rehabilitated," but merely argue that judgments in these cases are best made by other professions, possibly by sociology or law.

If my argument that mental illness exists and coerces the free will of an individual is persuasive, then the notion of limiting involuntary hospitalization and treatment merely to the dangerous makes no moral or logical sense. It is paradoxical and like arguing that the concussed victim should be treated if he is causing a nuisance, but otherwise ignored and left alone.

If mental illness does not exist, then there should be no intervention of any kind based on a therapeutic principle, and dangerous individuals should be put in jail. If it does exist, then all whose welfare and judgment are affected should be given the same constitutional benefits of treatment.

If it does not exist, then voluntary admissions cannot be tolerated either, if in any way the financial support is by society or insurance.

NOTES

1. For example, J. P. Leff, "Culture and the differentiation of emotional states," *British Journal of Psychiatry*, 123:299-307 (1973) and E. B. Wittkower, H. B. Murphy, J. Fried, and H. Ellenberger, "Cross-cultural inquiry into the Symptomatology of Schizophrenia," *Annals of the New York Academy of Sciences*, 84:854-863 (1960). E. B. Wittkower, "Perspectives of Transcultural Psychiatry," *International Journal of Psychiatry*, 8:811-824 (1969).

2. For a recent summary of the concepts underlying psychosomatic research see A. K. Gunderson, and R. H. Rahe, eds.; *Life Stress and Illness* (Springfield, Thomas, 1973). For the classic paper which started psychosomatic medicine in its current orientation, see F. Alexander, "Psychological Aspects of Medicine," *Psychosomatic Medicine*, 1:7-18 (1939). For an historical analysis of the interactions of psychological and physical factors, see H. I. Kaplan, and H. S. Kaplan, "A Historical Survey of Psychosomatic Medicine," *Journal of Nervous and Mental Diseases*, 124:546-568 (1956). For analysis by a Nobel Prize winner of the implications of interactions between host and invading organisms see R. J. Dubos, "Unsolved Problems in the Study and Control of Microbial Diseases," *Journal of American Medicine*, 157:1477-1479 (1955).

3. American Psychiatric Association: *Diagnostic and Statistical Manual of Mental Disorders*, 2nd ed. (DSMII). Published by the American Psychiatric Association, Washington, D. C., 1968. Prepared by the Committee on Nomenclature and Statistics. The introduction to this publication develops the history of the nosology and of the difficulties confronted by the American

psychiatric profession and the World Health Organization in its attempts to arrive at an internationally accepted nomenclature. The following is a direct quote:

> The first classification for mental disorders that was at all suitable for morbidity statistics was contained in the 6th revision of the International Classification of Diseases. This classification took into account much of the experience that had been gained in dealing with the many psychiatric casualties that occurred during World War II. Indeed, the rubrics in this classification were quite similar to those in the nomenclature of the Armed Forces of the United States (American Psychiatric Association, 1952).

4. Recently I was at a funeral service for a distinguished academician and the eulogy emphasized this man's brilliant dedication to a rather poorly known aspect of literary history. This scholar, one of the gentlest men in the literal meaning of that word, had dedicated much of his life to this study. By many value judgments, even the ones prevalent in the academic community, this was a study with poor pay-off, little prestige, comparatively minor possibilities for advancement. He was not aggressive, but withdrawn — a scholar for scholarship's sake! It is in such situations that the perjorative quality of labelling is most abhorrent to all of us. However, let me confront this with a patient presented at a psychiatric conference. This middle-aged lady had been admitted following a suicidal attempt or gesture. The history was of long periods of personal disabling physical illness coupled by a serious accident to the husband which impaired the financial stability of the family and threatened the loss of the home. In addition, the lady had serious difficulties with her oldest boy who was suffering from an incurable disease. She had attempted to get treatment at a local state psychiatric facility where she admitted herself voluntarily, but after a number of days was told that she was too healthy for the kind of care that they were able to give her. She struggled through for a couple of months and then made the suicidal gesture. The residents and psychology interns at the conference all agreed that she was in need of help, of encouragement, of counselling. There was a very distinct and not merely professionally induced division in the attitudes of the discussants whether the patient's reaction was pathological (that is, abnormal) or not. A number of the discussants argued that the set of circumstances faced by this lady made a reaction such as she suffered normal, expectable, and reasonable. Another group with which I was in agreement felt that the stresses, psychological and environmental, on this patient were so severe that no individual could have coped without some breakdown which had, in fact, occurred. I argued that the patient's reaction was pathological and abnormal, but that it was understandable in the context of the situation. The analogy here being that, given certain torsion of a foot in a skiing accident, even the healthiest athlete will suffer a broken bone; but no way can the broken bone be termed normal. However, I recognize both aspects of the argument. The main point that needs to be made is that mental illness and

abnormality are still seen by many as "bad" and as signs of weakness.

5. World Health Organization. *The International Pilot Study of Schizophrenia,* Vol. I, Geneva, 1973. The following is a direct quote with references: "Certainly, similar rates of schizophrenia have been reported from all over the world by investigators using both types of methods" (this refers to diagnostic criteria). The studies referred to are H. W. Dunham, *Community and Schizophrenia: an epidemiological analysis* (Detroit, *Wayne State University Press,* 1965). K. H. Fremming, "The Expectation of mental infirmity in a sample of the Danish Population," Occasional paper on eugenics #7, London, Cassell and the Eugenics Society, 1951.

6. See D. Rosenthal, and S. Kety, eds., *Transmission of Schizophrenia* (London and New York, Permagon Press, 1968). Also, the comprehensive study of W. Pollin, J. R. Stabenau, and J. Tupin, "Family Studies with Identical Twins discordant for Schizophrenia," *Psychiatry,* 28:60-78 (1965).

7. W. R. Gove, "Mental Illness, Societal Reaction as an explanation of Mental Illness: An evaluation," *American Sociological Review,* 35:873-883 (1973).

8. Due to the fact that the registry of occupations, births and deaths is centralized in England and Wales, it is comparatively easy to obtain information pertaining to the occupation of parents. Hence, the ease of doing meaningful epidemiological studies. J. Birtchnell, "Social Class, Parental Social Class and Social Mobility in Psychiatric Patients and general population controls," *Psychological Medicine,* 1:209-221 (1971). The only possible refutation of this finding could be that schizophrenia is a different entity in the British Isles than it is in the United States. However, a study which psychiatrists from both countries conducted in London and New York has found that, by and large, the statistics are comparable and the diagnostic criteria can be uniform J. E. Cooper, et al., *Psychiatric Diagnoses in New York and London: A comparative Study of Mental Hospital admissions* (Maudsley, monograph #20, New York, Oxford University Press, 1972).

9. L. Grinspoon, J. Ewalt, and R. Shader, *Schizophrenia: Pharmacotherapy and Psychotherapy* (Baltimore, Williams and Wilkins, 1972). Also P. R. A. May, *Treatment of Schizophrenia: A Comparative Study of Five Treatment Methods* (New York, Science House, 1968).

CHAPTER IV

CRITICISM AND ITS CHALLENGE

THE last twenty years have seen a tremendous, intensified and very articulate criticism of the practice of psychiatry in general and the practices of involuntary treatment for psychiatric illness in particular. The critics have come from within the psychiatric profession, from within the ranks of sociology and psychology, but perhaps the most challenging have been the criticisms coupled with court actions brought by the attorneys, particularly those associated with the New York and Washington branches of the American Civil Liberties Union.

The criticism has been general, specific, philosophical and ideological. Critics have assaulted the profession of psychiatry and have implied that its practices are close to those of quackery and that, therefore, it should be abolished. The president of the Psychological Society, in one of his annual presidential addresses, urged that psychiatry should be abolished and all psychiatrists made into family physicians. Academic and scholarly critics have, to their satisfaction and to the great discomfort of the psychiatric profession, proven that patients get better and get better quicker without psychotherapeutic intervention than with it. (1) Nader's group has assaulted the National Institute of Mental Health and its practices, challenging its role in the development of psychiatry and supervision of psychiatric health centers funded by federal monies. (2) The arguments have been general, but telling has been the specific contention that the majority of psychiatric practitioners embark on private office practice upon completing training where they treat the middle classes. The blacks and other minority groups have felt that psychiatrists have, by and large, failed to come to grips with the different problems of minority cultures, and that therefore the majority of psychiatrists have no skills or relevance in treating the black population. (3) This may be true, but it

64

condemns the individual, not the specialty! Women have accused psychiatrists of practicing sexually biased therapy evolving from elitist male chauvinist attitudes of Freudian psychoanalysis. (4) Sociologists enamoured with works such as Goffman's prove that psychiatrists indulge in empire building, and psychologists have flippantly said that psychiatrists spend their time training in medicine which they abandon to practice psychology which they have never studied.

Ultimately, the most serious criticisms and challenges have come from articulate political scientists and attorneys who have had the clout of legal intervention which, in many cases, they have used adroitly and (to be fair) with some general justification. Practices such as the peonage of psychiatric patients in state institutions have been brought to light and have been soundly condemned, since many patients are committed for treatment which is never delivered. (5)

Each of these criticisms needs to be discussed separately and analyzed in an objective, dispassionate manner, since many of the comments are pertinent and can only help the medical profession to improve its functioning and have a better understanding of its image and role in our society. The fact that occasionally the criticisms are uttered in ascerbic tones and at times by people who certainly would seem to lack academic or scholarly credibility should in no sense assuage or detract from the concerns that the medical profession should feel in regard to its practices. There is little question, however, that psychiatry as a profession, following what appeared to be two decades of glory and power which coincided with the psychopharmacological inventions in the 1950's and during which the Kennedy Bill of 1963 established community-oriented programs, has felt most seriously assaulted in recent years and has reacted in a very defensive fashion. Many academic institutions, not just psychiatry, have, in fact, oversold their product. The flagrant participation of academia in politics has not helped the academic community. Psychiatry as an intellectual and scholarly specialty was caught in the same "backlash," particularly since it could not deliver even a significant percentage of what had so hopefully and eagerly been promised and awaited. (6) Such criticism led in turn to a feeling on the part of psychiatrists of being assaulted by politicians and of being misunderstood by the political body in Washington. The ideological background of the majority of psychiatrists tends to be liberal, even possibly liberal-radical, and the Republican administration in office from 1968 made a ready scapegoat for many of the drying funds and apparent lack of understanding for psychiatric problems.

Yet while criticism mounted, many psychiatrists went about their business practicing excellent, mediocre or inadequate medicine as before; they were more concerned with the impact of the professional review organizations (P.S.R.O.) than with the general criticism of their everyday practices. (7) Patients continued to seek help, since no amount of criticism of the profession alleviates anxiety or depression. Many psychiatrists were trapped by their own ideological positions which are closely identified with the articulate spokesman of the ACLU and which they felt (or were) unable to directly confront. Too often their basic emotional loyalty is towards the same concerns for individual freedoms and political autonomy that the ACLU so articulately and vehemently argue. The cream of the profession are, furthermore, research-oriented or in psychoanalytic practice with few general hospital contacts or responsibilities. Money for research is an issue, but to be brutally frank, the budget of the local state hospital and commitment laws are of minor concern. (8)

Ultimately, and perhaps to his sorrow, the sickest psychiatric patient tends to be treated by the least experienced, the least competent psychiatrists. This is not peculiar to psychiatry; it is unfortunately a truism in medicine in general that emergency treatment is delivered by house staff (interns and residents) who have the least general knowledge or experience of their specialty. Many of the patients who are committed to psychiatric institutions are committed by overworked house staff in emergency rooms. The patients are brought, in the majority of cases, by various social agencies such as police officers, parole officers, public health nurses, etc. They are often indigent, inevitably poor, with few social or family ties (often referred to by psychiatry as "lifelines") in the community; the young, inexperienced staff physician, often burdened and tired after a day's work, reacts in the most opportunistic manner by initiating a commitment to the hospital. There are usually few opportunities for observation in the emergency room. The nursing staff wants the cases cleared and can make life very unpleasant for a young doctor.

It is a scandal that in a country of the affluence and wealth of the United States which prides itself on such excellent medical facilities and claims leadership in medicine the state psychiatric facilities can, at best, be described as medieval horrors and an offense to our civilization and a blot on psychiatry. While the last ten years have shown a steady and progressive decrease in the number of inmates, this has been accomplished by policies which are not free of criticism; while psychopharmacology made a definite impact, the revolving door policy was and is catastrophic! The patient is automatically discharged as soon as he is no longer acutely psychotic, but the discharge in most cases is to inadequate hospitals, convalescent homes, foster homes, boarding houses or welfare hotels. The follow-up facilities, which should have been provided by the community mental health centers, cannot afford to pay for medical help, so they employ social workers and psychologists who cannot prescribe medications, do not know how to deal with sick patients and concentrate on doing what they understand, such as family therapy, counselling, etc.

The state hospitals, once called asylums, are staffed by physicians who are grossly underpaid compared to what they could make in private practice. These hospitals are often the refuge of physicians who have come to this country from overseas to seek a better way of life. It would be unfair to state, as has been stated too often, that all physicians trained overseas are inadequate compared to those trained in the United States. Yet the fact of the matter is that only those who are unable to obtain a license in any state of the union or who, having obtained a license, for various quirks of personality feel more satisfaction in working in a state hospital, tend to continue in this area. There is, therefore, a selection process: those whose training, experience and motivation bring them on a par with the American-trained physician obtain their license and "move on," while those who are less able to compete on the American free market stay behind. Unfortunately, often these very same physicians may gravitate towards state psychiatric facilities because these facilities provide the majority of salaried jobs. The interest of such a physician may be in pediatrics or surgery, but salaried jobs are nonexistent in those areas (outside of Veterans' hosptials which require one license), and he seeks out opportunities in state psychiatric hospital facilities. Apart from their interest in psychiatry being minimal, their understanding of American mores, cultural differences, administrative and statutory rules is nonexistent. (9)

But the most serious criticism is their lack of ability to communicate. A surgeon may be able to obtain a good history through an interpreter and to do an excellent surgical procedure. A psychiatrist cannot. Language is his tool! I am particularly well aware of this, since a small percentage of patients at the University of Connecticut are non-English-speaking Puerto Ricans. I have at times been asked to do psychiatric evaluations on them, and for many years I felt it my moral and medical obligation to attempt to do this. I am now convinced that my participation in such an exercise is sheer hypocrisy in that through the interpreter I cannot possibly understand the nuances and problems which could lead to a legitimate psychiatric conclusion. Therefore, I think the patient and his primary doctor have more to gain by being confronted by the fact that they can only make a judgment on the basis of what passes for a psychiatric evaluation.

This same holds true for many psychiatrists from foreign countries, particularly from the Asian ones (Indians, Philippinos, Koreans) who have flocked to this country. Furthermore, and this is no criticism of these physicians, their attitude toward the patients is often a direct result of their own cultural attributes. They are often of middle and upper class backgrounds, the elite of their own societies where class differences tend to be if not more marked than in this country, at least articulated and perceived quite differently. They take a rather condescending and authoritarian position towards the inmates.

I have sketched a general background of some of the criticisms directed at the psychiatric profession, but I wish to emphasize that criticism is not a recent discovery of the American Civil Liberties Union. The criticism and constant soul searching of the medical profession and of the psychiatric specialty in this area has a long history. A review of the literature certainly indicates that many methods have been tried to enhance the availability of necessary treatment as well as to preserve the freedom of the individual.

It is a well-accepted adage, and I think an empirical truth, that if a problem has many cures and many different explanations, it means that it is poorly understood and complex. Possibly it means that the answers and implementation are complex, expensive and unpopular. The concern about commitment is an excellent example of this, and a review of the literature, however brief, illustrates the struggle between the two polarized positions. The United States, with its variety of different jurisdictions, is a veritable potpourri of ever-changing rules and regulations, policies and concerns. Constant appeals are made for uniformity, commissions are formed to study the problem, reports are written and presented, arguments are advanced, and truisms are reiterated.

Many of the studies lack historical objectivity and repeat or perpetuate the most simplistic concepts of the evolution of civil law. The *Harvard Law Review* ("Civil Commitment of the Mentally Ill: Theories and Procedures") comes up with the conclusion that "in the 19th century, the mentally ill first came to be seen as sick, rather than cursed and as susceptible to aid through proper treatment." (10) Certainly in the English jurisdiction which is of the most direct historical pertinence to the traditions and practices of the United States, there are many well established evidences of the recognition of lunacy and insanity. But the very fact that these practices of hospitalizing the mentally ill go back so many centuries is also reflected in many concerns which have to do with the protection of civil rights, the protection of inherent human dignity of the patient once he is hospitalized.

There has been an atavistic concern and a fear in the community of being "railroaded." Curran, in his paper, addresses this, but the amount of evidence which would really document such facts is, by and large, rather scanty. (11) The laws of England, however, did allow those responsible for the indigent pauper an inordinate amount of control over his behavior. But even the rich occasionally were subject to what is now popularly referred to as a "railroading process," and that case of Alexander Cruden was actually published in 1739 as "The story of a London citizen exceedingly injured: or a British inquisition displayed in an account of the unparalleled case of a citizen of London, book seller to the late Queen who was sent to a private madhouse." (12) This practice of private madhouses eventually led to the lunacy laws which stated most forcibly that only institutions which were examined by the Lunacy Commission could take inmates for money. This Act of 1774 provided for licensing and inspection of private madhouses and required a medical certificate for admission; in 1800 a new Act addressed itself to the very questions that are of such pertinence today, such as the potential unlawful detention of sane people, the maltreatment of inmates, the need for good hospital accommodation for the large number of insane paupers who were neglected and finally, the separation of the criminal lunatic from the ordinary lunatic. Some of these recommendations were implemented in a program of building asylums throughout the country. But way back over a hundred years ago the concern was the same as now — concern for the preservation of freedom, the right to treatment, patients' rights, and the destigmatizing of the mentally ill.

In 1815 in Britain, a Parliamentary inquiry into madhouses took place which raised the most serious criticism of the situation that existed in even the well-known hospitals such as the Royal Bethlehem Institute. In this report, the Parliament was given a statement in which the examiners saw a man of fifty-five confined in a lower gallery for fourteen years who, because of the consequences of attempting to defend himself, was fastened by a long chain which enabled the keeper to draw him to the wall at pleasure. Certainly, the Commission was horrified at what they found in these institutions. This activated the British Parliament in 1845 to pass an act to undo many of these evils. Rules for the regulation and treatment of lunatics were promulgated and the laws for the provision and regulation of lunatic asylums for counties and boroughs were amended. A new Commission was created called the Commission on Lunacy to oversee the acts and most strongly endorsed the moral treatment (of Tuke) and recommended humanitarian conditions in the asylums which were sadly lacking. (13)

In the United States Dorothea Linder Dix, 1802 to 1887, also urged a positive approach to the mentally ill. After spending some time with Samuel Tuke at York, she dedicated her life towards the improvement of the conditions of the mentally ill in the asylums of the United States. Her interventions in the British Isles led to the introduction of a lunacy act for Scotland prefaced by a remark of the Earl of Shaftsbury, Chancellor of England, who states that, "I believe that not in any country in Europe nor in any part of America is there any place in which pauper lunatics are in such suffering and degraded state as those in Her Majesty's Kingdom of Scotland." The concern for civil rights did not escape the medical profession either. A Dr. Diller of Pittsburgh, Pennsylvania wrote that, "In looking over the commitment laws of the various states, they appear to me in general to be cumbersome and unwieldy and in some cases as in Pennsylvania to insufficiently guard personal liberty and protect the certifying physicians." (14) Dr. Diller discusses the variety of laws pertaining to the involuntary treatment of the mentally ill, a situation which certainly has not changed for the better in the last sixty years, and praises Connecticut, New York and Massachusetts for their progressive statutes which enable the violently insane to be treated as a psychiatric emergency and which, at the same time, protect the civil liberties of the individual. He particularly condemns the Commonwealth of Pennsylvania where, at that time, two physicians were able to make an indefinite commitment of an individual.

Doctor Diller furthermore states that,

> since the law regards as one of the most precious and fundamental rights of all citizens personal liberty, the law should not permit such liberty to be taken from any citizen except by due process of law and then upon official order by a judge of the court. No one should be deprived of his liberty for any cause whatsoever except bye process of law and by action

of the court, and this rule should apply to the deprivation of liberty on account of insanity as well as crime.

He recommends that

Pennsylvania's statutes should be changed to conform to the fundamental law of the land and of the majority of the states which require that commitment shall be made only by a judge of the court after due investigation which should include the testimony of two physicians made after examination of the person in question who should always have a chance to contest the commitment.

That is strong language and certainly antedates much of the current furor. Incidentally, Dr. Diller, in the same paper, states a rather interesting position:

Voluntary commitment of insane persons by themselves is an anomaly and cannot stand logical and legal scrutiny.

Dr. Diller also strongly condemns voluntary admission to asylums:

A man who is sound mentally may make a reasonable contract, but if a man is insane it is a farce and against all rules of logic to permit him to make a written contract depriving himself of his liberty.

Again, the issue of competence, of informed consent, is raised in perhaps rather extreme fashion.

In an article in *The Medical Record* by Dr. Atwood, a review of a number of cases discharged from insane asylums is outlined and the results of each are discussed. (15)

Dr. Chapin, in *The American Journal of Insanity,* October, 1892, appealed for unification of state laws. If "railroading" and civil rights was even then an issue, so was the medical man's response to this — a documentation of facts which proved that this was a rare occurrence. (16) Following Mrs. Packard's impassioned appeal against the rule of hospitalizing wives at behest of the husbands, a commission investigated all Illinois state asylums and found no case of unwarranted admission. In fact, there is good evidence that she, herself, was indeed mentally ill. Lord Shaftsbury, before the Special Commission of Parliament and Lunacy Laws in 1877 stated,

I am ready enough to believe that when temptation gets hold of a man's heart, he is capable of anything. But I am happy to say providence throws so many difficulties in the way of these conspiracies, that I believe conspiracies in 99 cases out of 100 to be altogether impossible. The number of certificates that have passed through our offices in 1859 amount to more than 185,000 and of all of those certificates, I do not think so many as half a dozen have been found defective. (17)

The following statement from Dr. Blumer, in a paper presented at the Fourth Session of the International Congress of Charities, Correction and Philanthropy, Chicago, 1893 entitled "The Commitment, Detention, Care and Treatment of the Insane in America" states:

Too much of our legislation seems to be based on the assumption of improper motives on the parts of friends and relatives as if it were to be expected that cruelty and inhumanity instead of being the rare exception should be the normal rule and state of things in civilized society.

The analogy of those days with current issues of informed consent and reasonable treatment finds its parallel in the statement by Mr. Clifford Allbut in 1891 in "The Proposed Hospitals for the Treatment of the Insane." Allbut's conclusion was that,

The fact is the desire to reinstate treatment by medicine is a retrograde tendency. Modern therapeutics (of psychiatric patients) are marked not by the multiplication of medicines but by a gradual restriction of their field. (18)

The point of this historical outline is again to illustrate that the wheel has not been recently discovered, that many of the concerns which are being articulated now have been voiced in the past, and the fact that certain concerns and the practices which raise these concerns continue and are indications that the problems cannot be wiped out by redefinitions or necessarily by ideological statements.

The challenge of the criticism, however, is that it continually forces the profession to look to itself for greater skill and precision in its language and in the treatment modalities that it delivers. If there is one thing that psychiatry, as part of medicine, can take pride in, it is its humility and willingness to incorporate into its practices lessons learned from experience. The criticism, therefore, that is currently being propounded, follows the arguments which can be summarized as: Mental illness does not exist, and psychiatric nosology is merely a verbal description of behavior and conduct. All behavior is under volitional control. All citizens have a right to behave and conduct their activities along the lines that they please as long as they are not in direct confrontation with social goals. Freedom and liberty are so precious that nothing should deprive an individual of them unless it can be proven that his conduct is physically dangerous to others. Psychiatrists are poor prognosticators of dangerousness and, therefore, detention for dangerousness should be a criminal proceeding and not a psychiatric issue.

Behavior that is considered to be a form of psychiatric illness is merely one of various forms of deviancy which society has chosen to label with the stigma of illness. There is no way of diagnosing mental illness through factual organic evidence and, therefore, people who are so labeled become exposed to various forms of repression by society. An example of this may very well be homosexuality.

Hospitalization of psychiatric patients leads to a form of institutionalization which, in turn, develops and accentuates patterns of social inadequacy, chronicity and withdrawal.

The issue of insisting on involuntary hospitalization of people is so abhorrent to society and so contrary to the rights that are guaranteed in the constitution that this may not, under any circumstance, be left exclusively to physicians, however well-trained and however well-meaning.

If patients need to be hospitalized, they can only be involuntarily committed to institutions which provide quality psychiatric treatment compatible with their needs. Since many facilities fail to come up to the standards, however minimal, espoused by the American Psychiatric Association, involuntary commitment is an abridgment of certain rights without the provision of the service for which the right has been in fact abridged.

The keystone to the issue of autonomy and the practice of involuntary hospitalization of certain people for mental illness has to do with the acceptance and the definition of the concept of mental illness. If this can be accepted and criteria validated, then much argument disappears. If, indeed, this is merely a definitional term for behavior which some of the members of our society consider to be deviant and therefore objectionable, and if this conduct is under some form of volitional control, then the whole model for psychiatric involuntary hospitalization falls apart, and in fact should be abandoned.

This point has been argued in Chapter III. If the evidence that mental illness exists is not beyond a reasonable doubt then the whole process of involuntary treatment stands assaulted on its basic principle. If however, the possibility of mental illness as an operational construct remains, but the only argument is *the extent* to which it affects the volitional judgment, then certain responsibilities and safeguards have to be accepted and criticisms faced. The conclusion would be that criticisms should modify the practices and work for *maximizing* effectiveness of treatment and *minimizing* abuse.

Furthermore, it is often forgotten that even those who accept the medical model of mental disease (e.g. schizophrenia) also accept the medical fact that the severity and incapacitating aspects of the illness will vary between different individuals depending on a whole variety of social and psychological factors. Even in the same individual, symptoms will vary from day to day, as do the pains of arthritis.

The attorney brings in the philosophy of criminal law: innocent until proven guilty, therefore free of mental illness until proven to have it! There are no basic differences in guilt, though punishments and correctional approaches vary. The attorney applies this static model to mental illness. It is either there or not, and there are not variations within it. If it is present on Wednesday and not readily perceived on Sunday, then the expert has made a mistake either on Wednesday or Sunday or both, but it is seldom accepted that both observations may be correct.

Many criticisms of the involuntary process are made by attorneys, who tend to mix their arguments and who short-change their own scholarliness by indulging in a mixture of arguments which, at times, are paradoxical if not contradictory. Arguments are postulated that mental illness does not exist; at the same time, "legal" points are scored by stating that putting people in hospitals makes them worse. The question that can well be asked is, "What makes them worse?" or "In what way are they worse?" if mental illness does not exist? Is it their conduct, their personality or their adaptiveness that is made worse or decreased? Many attorneys, if not the majority who are involved in this area, argue that the process of involuntary hospitalization should be limited only to those who are dangerous. Then with a certain amount of accuracy, if not always of good taste, they point out that psychiatrists are poor prognosticators of dangerousness. If mental illness exists and affects judgment or autonomy, then to limit treatment to the dangerous is like saying, "Only the belligerent victim of an accident will be treated." The quiet and unconscious ones will be allowed to lie and die, since they cause no trouble and since they cannot give informed consent. If mental illness does not affect the executive ego of the individual, then indeed it is an offense to treat such a person and to modify his behavior — at least, it is offensive in our current cultural and political context.

In this respect, Dr. Szasz is consistent. (19) While I cannot possibly agree with his dogmatic denial of the existence of mental illness or the corollary that all individuals have equal ability for making decisions about their lives, at least he is uniformly consistent in his position. He denies the existence of mental illness, and he, therefore, is against commitment. He is against *all* commitment. The argument that societal intervention is appropriate when the individual is suffering from conduct described as a combination of dangerousness and mental illness asks psychiatry and psychiatrists to do exactly what they have been most castigated for allegedly doing — namely, being agents of the establishment.

Assuming that the criticisms of psychiatric medical commitment are made in good faith rather than in an ideological manner, it is interesting to analyze the points and see if they are applicable, if they hold together and if they make any sense.

Lawyers continually argue the benefits of arriving at the truth by an adversary process, so let us discuss the points that are made in the New York Civil Liberties Union Legislative memo which emanates from the most active civil liberties group in the country and one that has been most articulate in denouncing involuntary hospitalization. In this memo, the New York Civil Liberties Union (N.Y.C.L.U.), through its Board of Directors, makes the following statements: (20) "Mental illness can never, by itself, be a justifiable reason for depriving a person of liberty of property, against his objection." Now the only response to that is, Why Not?

The N.Y.C.L.U. assures us that only one third of state hospital admissions in New York State are involuntary; therefore, not too many people would be affected. Furthermore, of course, they quote John Stuart Mill. Strangely enough, they refrain from quoting the constitution. However, the constitution is very often quoted, though in this case the N.Y.C.L.U. has managed to realize a certain inappropriateness in the historical sequence. The critics who do pull in the constitution point out that often Article V is invoked which states that:

> nor shall any person be subject for the same offense to be twice put into jeopardy of life or limb nor shall be compelled in any criminal case to be a witness against himself; nor be deprived of life, liberty or property, without due process of law; nor shall private property be taken for public use without just compensation.

This article most clearly refers to criminal matters, and historically, at that time, the ease with which people *were* incarcerated in psychiatric institutions or asylums, clearly negates the possibility that the founding fathers were thinking of protecting the right of the mentally ill to their mental illness.

But going to the N.Y.C.L.U., the authors of that document get around this by stating that,

> We should be *especially* solicitous of liberty when liberty rests on a concept so inprecise as mental illness. Unlike tuberculosis or cancer, mental illness is not a cause of disorder; it is at most a theory.

The authors manage, here, to bring in an argument that has

found favor in a much more scholarly and honestly written document — namely, the one by Livermore, et al. Livermore writes, (21)

> The tradition for involuntary treatment of the mentally ill while voluntary for other kinds of illness (e.g. cancer) is that the mentally ill are incapable of making rational judgments of whether they need or desire such help. This depends on what kind of mental illness is present. It is likely that a pederast understands that society views him as sick, that certain kinds of psychiatric treatment may cure him, and that such treatment is available in certain mental institutions.

This is a reasonable, in fact, a most significant criticism of the looseness of the concept of mental illness; that it has been abused by society in general and even by the psychiatric profession is beyond any question. My children refer to individuals who exhibit certain behaviors as "sickies." Psychiatrists refer to certain forms of conduct as pathological, as needing to be treated. No question but that too much is subsumed under this rather loose concept. I can only speak for myself and hold fast to what I outlined in Chapter III. But this reasonable criticism stemming from Livermore is not made by the N.Y.C.L.U. They become quite personal about it and state,

> Some psychiatrists, for example, believe that all hippies are mentally ill; others disagree. Human liberty, however, should not depend on diagnostic bias.

A doubt is planted in the mind of the reader. He already begins to conceptualize an establishment-oriented, middle-aged individual viewing with disapproval the behavior of marijuana-smoking, long-haired, radical youth. The next step that is perceived, obviously, is wholesale commitment and possible psychosurgery, or at least behavior modification and haircut!

It is unfortunate that that argument was not left to stand; it had a certain emotional impact. N.Y.C.L.U. states, however, that "furthermore, even if a thousand psychiatrists agreed that a given person was mentally ill (and nondangerous) that would not justify admission." They furthermore state that the assumption made for such practice is that such a patient "is incompetent to make a rational choice between liberty or treatment and second, he would, if competent, choose treatment. There is not, however, any evidence to support either of these assumptions." They refrain from admitting there is no evidence to the contrary!

It is rather interesting that the authors conceptualize the struggle of liberty versus treatment; that, apparently, is their perception of the alternatives. They do not for a second consider the possibility that a sick schizophrenic living in a delusional world of his anxieties and fears is not at liberty. They make a very interesting assumption. They accuse psychiatrists of assuming that were a patient to make a rational choice, he would wish to be free of his anxieties and free of his illness; the N.Y.C.L.U. appear to assume the contrary — that a psychotic, troubled individual would prefer to stay that way rather than to get better. To them, there are no degrees of illness. Apparently, either people are so ill that they might be incompetent or they are so well that they make rational choices.

"There is growing recognition that mental illness and incompetence are not synonymous and that many persons who are mentally ill are entirely competent to make rational and important decisions concerning their affairs, including the decision to accept or reject hospital treatment. There are thousands of mentally ill persons who acknowledge their mental illness and voluntarily apply for treatment."

I concur completely with the statement that mental illness and incompetence are not synonymous. Having concurred with that, the obvious logic is that the severity of impairment in some people precludes their making rational decisions, while some are able to do so. But what makes people incompetent — lack of competence? Having discounted in the beginning the possibility of the existence of mental illness and the fact that it is *never* by itself a justifiable reason for depriving a person of liberty, the N.Y.C.L.U. then make a rather paradoxical argument:

"Some types of mental illness are not treatable at all and even for those types that are treatable, the probability that a given patient will be permanently cured or even improved because of the treatment is discouragingly low. Of course, a good number of patients admitted to mental hospitals are released as 'improved' within a matter of months, but most of them (over 50%) return.

Also, there is very little hard evidence that even temporary improvement is the result of treatment and is not, instead, a spontaneous remission." The authors cite a study which allegedly proves that 50 percent of all patients with schizophrenia recover without treatment! Having cited the study that 50 percent recover spontaneously, it is paradoxical in terms of the fact that some types of mental illness which do "not exist" are not treatable (i.e. some are?), that the probability is that many people suffering from a theoretical construct will not be cured, but that they would get better anyway from whatever they didn't have and that, unfortunately, 50 percent of them will return, having become imbued with "unconventional conduct," "belief" or "theory"!

In view of my conviction that mental illness does exist, that it can be diagnosed and that it can be treated, let us see if we can treat the remarks somewhat more seriously. It is a matter of record (See Chap. III) that people with mental illness in the majority of cases can be treated, that they do get better, that the improvement is not a change of their personality to something different, but an improvement back to their previous optimum state of functioning and that their readmission is in *most* instances related to acute stresses and discontinuation of medication. (22)

The point about temporary improvement being a natural remission and not due to treatment is somewhat problematical in that many patients with minimal or no antipsychotic medications, if removed from the stresses of their lives, do get better. Ths is also true for patients with acute peptic ulcers who, when they are hospitalized and treated in a most conservative manner and given rest and a tension-free situation, also improve. The ulcer heals, the bleeding stops, the pain disappears. These people also get sick again.

The authors, of course, bring in the case of the unfortunate late and respected Justice Robert Jackson who allegedly had a heart attack, was allegedly told by his physician that he should not go back to work, which he proceeded to do and which allegedly caused him to die. Assuming that all these points are completely correct, one can only say that unless the judge had his brain in his heart, the analogy does not hold true and that it is another one of these rather emotional arguments which cannot stand scrutiny.

The N.Y.C.L.U. further states that even "short term hospitalization can of itself reinforce and exacerbate some types of mental illness and that long term hospitalization is particularly anti-therapeutic." I think the opperative phrase here is "some types of mental illness." If I had a broken bone from a skiing accident, I certainly hope that I would not be referred to an ophthalmologist for a retinal operation, and, indeed, if I had to undergo a serious surgical operation, I certainly would hope that I would not be put in with patients suffering with infectious diseases. I think the question here is: "What is appropriate for what kind of problem?"

If the authors imply that the facilities to which the majority of people are committed are grossly and scandalously inadequate, then I concur, and this has been established in lawsuits and in medical literature. If we accept the fact that emergency services for accident victims on American highways are scandalously inadequate compared to the services provided to the American military personnel in the Southeastern Asia conflict and compared to what potentially could be provided if there were a will in implementing such programs, then it is like saying that highway victims should be left to die in peace because they so often get such lousy care.

The authors of the N.Y.C.L.U. document then make a telling point. Having to their satisfaction proven that only the dangerous and mentally ill should be committed, they then argue against themselves by stating,

> Of all the identifiable dangerous groups in society, only the mentally ill are singled for preventive detention and they are probably the least dangerous, as a group, of the groups here mentioned. Why should society confine a person if he is dangerous and mentally ill but not if he is dangerous and sane?

Why, Indeed? I agree. And it makes no sense, but neither does the next point the authors make.

> Courts have difficulty enough in deciding whether a past act under known circumstances was the product of a mental disease, or was instead the product of cultural, educational, economic, familial or other factors. Psychiatrists have not been very helpful in that regard, and it is both naive and

disingenuous to assume they can be more helpful in predicting whether an unspecified future act, under unknown circumstances, will be the product of a mental disease.

I can only say that the fantasy of this document escapes all inherent logic. The psychiatrist is told he can, under no circumstance, commit, unless he finds the individual mentally ill (a condition which does not exist) and dangerous. Such cases do happen, though they are rare, but I have seen dangerous (and mentally ill) individuals in the emergency room. But the authors make a point of ignoring the possibility of present danger and infer that only future danger is being discussed or considered. But the cat is out of the bag with this statement:

> Proponents of civil confinement of the mentally ill quite correctly argue that abolition of involuntary confinement would cause much human degradation and social harm, but less, perhaps, than its retention.

In the body of the document, the authors quote the high percentage of voluntary admissions to English psychiatric facilities. Even Szasz's point which is that voluntary admission is a fraud and that coercion is used in many cases does not hold; then we should ask ourselves, why the difference? (23)

Are the English so stupid that they believe more readily in a construct, a theoretical explanation for behavior which does not exist? Is the level of their mental illness such that they are more competent to make decisions? Are their facilities more pleasing and attractive? Is their society conceivably more homogeneous and the trust in a physician's recommendation greater?

The authors accept the possibility of much human degradation and social harm. I wonder if they realize that this social harm and degradation will affect the most disadvantaged and the most underprivileged members of society.

Quite independently of the ideological position advocated by the N.Y.C.L.U., there is the concern of many, including distinguished members of the psychiatric profession, that the field and the profession of psychiatry will be abused for political and thus repressive ends. Quite frequently, examples from the Soviet Union are cited which tend to illustrate this danger. (24)

The whole area of thought control is becoming more of a

reality, hence the concern is closer to all of us. Problems about computerized storage date banks and invasion of privacy are no longer myths of scientific futuristic novelists, but realities of the present day. Many people fail to perceive the qualitative difference between psychosurgery performed to modify behavior in attitudes and the treatment of a suicidal depressive psychotic with electric-convulsive therapy. Even those who are able to accept the fact that in one case, for whatever bad or good social ends, intrusion on an individual is performed to modify his behavior and thus to change him, often cannot understand the fact that this *is not* the same as a treatment done to bring him back to the situation he was in before, and they still articulate and fear dangers of abuse.

Psychiatry is, undoubtedly, guilty of many of the offenses with which it is charged. Grandiose, it sought to establish its influence over the law in its explanations for criminal behavior. It sought to establish its influence over government and international politics. (25)

A number of years ago I was looking at, and in turn being looked over for, a position as a director of a student mental health clinic. I heard the following words of advice from one of the members of the search committee. Paraphrased, the comment suggested that I should establish a positive contact with the student body, become aware of their problems and their aspirations and act as their advocate in regard to the dean's office. In other words, I was told I should keep in mind the position of Reverend Coffin at Yale. There was no advice or interest in my expertise of treating the disturbed students or even in working to modify those deleterious social influences on the campus which preclude the full flowering of social and intellectual maturity in the student.

Many psychiatrists have identified themselves very strongly with such aspirations. Psychiatry has to learn that its language is subject to serious misinterpretation. Too often at parties people make remarks directed to the fact that I must be observing and analyzing their behavior and their thoughts. These remarks are made in jest, but there is always a certain grain of concern behind them. It may be unkind and bad mannered for my high school daughter to refer to a teacher as a real "sickie," but it raises serious questions of common sense if I do the same.

Psychiatry should be very clear as to the problems that it claims specific competence in treating and diagnosing. The movement of psychoanalytic psychology, so fruitful in advancing the understanding of human behavior, should not be allowed to be synonymous with psychiatry. Yet for countless people, even very educated ones, the difference between a psychiatrist, a psychologist and a psychoanalyst is, at best, vague or unclear. For many students, psychiatry began with Freud, and all psychoanalysts are psychiatrists, and vice versa.

The critics of psychiatry should also bear in mind that in those countries or in those situations in which psychiatry has been subverted for political ends, the political parties and the judiciary have been subverted first and have been the initiators of the subversion. Those in the profession who identify themselves with a radical movement, who would turn away from treating the patient to treating and modifying society bring no joy or comfort to the profession.

I am only too willing to admit that the political naivete of the profession and its particular and specific concern, human and interpersonal relationships, make it both an obvious victim and at times a ready one for exploitation and subversion, and care and vigilance have to be continually exercised to prevent abuse. But abuse has to be guarded against in life politics, professional and social.

The concern here is so articulate, so vehement that it poses the obvious question: is it merely an American phenomenon?

NOTES

1. H. J. Eysenck, "Behavior Therapy, Spontaneous remission and transference in Neurotics," *American Journal of Psychiatry*, 119:867-871 (1963). Professor Eysenck, from London, internationally known psychologist and exponent of behavior modification techniques as well as very scholarly and persuasive critic of psychoanalysis and its derivitives such as psychotherapy has forcefully and frequently documented the questionable nature of improvement achieved in neurotics by psychotherapy. However, in Chapter III we made a point of definitely excluding the fact of neurotic behavior as being a mental illness even

though as an adaptational style of life, it may be quite incapacitating. Therefore, critics of commitment who quote Professor Eysenck and his very challenging conclusions to establish a point that psychiatric treatment is ineffective, are, at best, prey of academic ignorance or, at worst, guilty of academic dishonesty. Neurotics are not, by and large, committed to institutions and there is sufficient and overwhelming evidence that psychiatric treatment is successful with mentally ill, psychotic individuals. See footnote #9 in Chapter III.

2. F. D. Chu, "The Nader Report: One author's perspective," *American Journal of Psychiatry*, 131:775-779 (1974) followed by comments of Doctors Farnsworth, Marmor and Cole, pages 779-782. Also F. D. Chu, and S. Crotter, *The Madness Establishment* (New York, Grossman, 1974).

3. J. Agel, ed. *The Radical Therapist* (New York, Valentine Books, 1971).

4. P. Chessler, *Women and Madness* (Garden City, Doubleday & Company, 1972).

5. Actions are now being brought against state institutions by patients alleging that during their stay as committed involuntary residents, they were either forced or, at best, forcefully encouraged to work for no financial remuneration. Currently the most notable is the case of Mrs. Rita Dale, reported in *Psychiatric News* (September 20th, 1972) discussed in R. Slovenko, *Law and Psychiatry* (New York, Basic Books, 1973), Chapter XIV — "Rights of committed patients."

6. For a forthright and constructive criticism free of diatribes and polemics, see R. R. Grinker, "Psychiatry rides madly in all directions," *Archives of General Psychiatry*, 10:228-237 (1964). Also L. Eisenberg, "The future of Psychiatry," *Lancet*, 1371-1375 (1973). D. X. Freedman, and R. P. Gordon, "Psychiatry under Siege: Attacks from Without," *Psychiatric Annals*, 3:10-34 (1973).

7. Federal Public Act 92-603 mandating the professional standards review organization (P.S.R.O.). The very serious abuses by some private practitioners of federal insurance, particularly, Medicare and Medicaid, led to an understandable concern and a wish to curtail unnecessary treatments and length of stay in hospital. As part of the amendment to the Social Security Act, this public law will impose a review of all patient care done in a hospital setting. One can only say that the medical profession in the United States brought this on itself. On the other hand, the amount of money and time that will now go towards these reviews will probably be greater than the amount saved by control of a few unscrupulous practitioners. Hopefully, however, the quality of care of all patients will be increased. This form of peer review appears to be a uniquely American experience.

8. Statement in the *Psycho-Analytic Review*, 58:385-394 (1971), Dr. Ernestine R.

Haight writes as follows: "I refer to the New York Civil Liberties Union which, on equalitarian and democratic grounds, has endorsed the psychoanalytic view — opposition to involuntary confinement." I do not know how much this view reflects the majority attitude of psychoanalysts, but I am quite convinced that most of them wish psychoanalytic treatment to be covered by medical insurance and thus view it as a *medical* illness. In the study done on attitudes of psychiatrists towards commitment, a number of psychoanalysts did not respond, pleading lack of experience with "ward" cases. Also see A. A. Rogow, *The Psychiatrists* (New York, G. P. Putnam & Sons, 1970).

9. See note #16, Chapter II. Background on Foreign Medical Graduates.

10. "Civil Commitment of the Mentally Ill: Theories and Procedures," *Harvard Law Review*, 79:1288-1298 (1966).

11. W. J. Curran, "Hospitalization of the Mentally Ill," *North Carolina Law Review*, 31:274-298 (1967). Discusses the development in the early years of the republic of special legislation towards the restraint of "the furiously mad." The tremendous agitation around the case of Mrs. Packard (see R. Dewey, "The Jury Law for Commitment of the Insane in Illinois (1867-1893) and Mrs. E.P.W. Packard, its author; also later developments in Lunacy Legislation in Illinois," *American Journal of Insanity*, 69:571-584 (1913), Chapter I and the publication by Charles Read of a book called *Hard Cash* in 1860 describing the "railroading" of a young man, were all grist for the mill of public concern. Professor Curran, as well as Dr. Deutsch, *The Mentally Ill in America* (New York, Columbia University Press, 1949), credit the situations with the beginning of jury trial legislation for mental illness and a serious popular concern about incarceration in mental institutions: W. R. Dunton, "Mrs. Packard and Her Influence upon Laws for the Commitment of the Insane," *Johns Hopkins Bulletin*, 18:419-424 (1907).

12. This is described in R. Hunter, and I. MacAlpine, *Three Hundred Years of Psychiatry: 1535-1860* (London, Oxford University Press, 1963).

13. The developments discussed are outlined with direct quotes from the appropriate parliamentary commissions and investigations in R. Hunter, and I. MacAlpine, *Three Hundred Years of Psychiatry: 1535-1860*, supra footnote #12.

14. T. Diller, "Commitment of the Insane in the United States," *Illinois Medical Journal*, 26:322-324 (1914).

15. C. E. Atwood, "A Review of some of the cases in which insane persons have been released from custody by the courts within the past six years," *Medical Record*, 48:113-116 (1898). This paper deals with "All the male patients who have been discharged by the courts from the hospital with which I (i.e. Dr.

Atwood) have been connected during the past six years." Dr. Atwood discusses a number of cases which were released by the courts from psychiatric custody and quotes a member of the state commission on lunacy who allegedly stated that in all of his experience he had never met a case of illegal detention.

16. J. B. Chapin, "On the Detention of the Insane, and the writ of habeas corpus," *American Journal of Insanity*, 53:242-255 (1896-1897). Dr. Chapin, in this paper, presents a record of a number of individuals who pleaded the habeas corpus proceeding and states, "It should be especially noted that with one exception, the mental condition of these persons was so apparent in the courtroom that the judges had no difficulty, without the opinion of the physician, in arriving at a conclusion. Some of the persons exhibited pleasure at the display of their delusions, but their lawyers engaged in the cases expressed their own opinion of perfect sanity of the clients, making no account of the distress occasioned by the publication of their unfortunate condition."

17. J. A. Blumer, "The Commitment, Detention, Care and Treatment of the Insane in America." In J. A. Blumer, and A. B. Richardson (Ed.), *International Congress of Charities, Corrections and Philanthropy*. (Baltimore, Johns Hopkins, 1894). In this paper Dr. Blumer quotes Lord Shaftsbury. He also quotes Dr. Stephen Smith and his paper before a national conference of charities who urged more unification of state laws.

18. J. A. Blumer, "Commitment, Detention, Care and Treatment of the Insane in America," see supra footnote#17. Also quotes Dr. Clifford Albut in his statements made to the London County Council. Apparently reported but not verified by me in the *Journal of Mental Science* (October, 1891).

19. T. S. Szasz, *Law, Liberty and Psychiatry*. (New York, MacMillan & Company, 1963).

20. New York Civil Liberties Union Legislative Memo. #1, obtainable from 56 Fifth Avenue, New York. Also published in the *Psychoanalytic Review*, 58:385 394 (1971). also see footnote #14, Chapter I.

21. J. M. Livermore, et al., "On the Justification for Civil Commitment," *University of Pennsylvania Law Review*, 117:75-96 (1968).

22. See footnote #9, Chapter III.

23. T. S. Szasz, "Voluntary Mental Hospitalization, an unacknowledged practice of medical fraud," *New England Journal of Medicine*, 287:277-278 (1972).

24. R. A. Medvedev, and Z. Medvedev, *A Question of Madness*. (New York,

Random House, 1972).

25. See footnote #5, Chapter II.

CHAPTER V

A UNIQUELY AMERICAN PROBLEM?

WHAT is it about the American system that has so particularly accentuated the concern about involuntary treatment and hospitalization? Why is it that the issue of involuntary commitment, which in the rest of the civilized world is accepted as a medical matter, has raised so much legal concern in the United States? What is peculiar to the United States, its social climate, political system or societal concerns which has led intelligent and educated people to not merely question the potential abuses of the system, the inequities of application of the system and potentially the inequities of right to treatment, but to actually deny the very concept of mental illness and disease?

Is democracy, love of freedom so much more advanced? Are the Europeans such willing dupes of the medical profession? Is medicine in Europe endowed with greater trust?

These are some of the questions that cannot be ignored, even though answers are difficult to come by!

Interestingly enough, the difference in the basic approach to the problem between Europe and the United States is one that may answer and prognosticate the future developments in this conflicted area. The level of medical sophistication in both continents is comparable. Possibly, the United States is technologically a generation ahead of Europe, while the Europeans appear to lead in community programs, preventive care and comprehensive medical insurance. But these differences are differences of social concern, not of basic knowledge or potential application. So the differences in involuntary commitment practices reflect such basic and cultural contexts as the trust of the community in the physician or in the judge. They reflect, furthermore, the social goals of the community and the ultimate sense of purpose of that community.

There are so many common attributes and shared goals and

styles of life between Europe and the United States that some of
the fundamental differences are often ignored or not recognized.

The nations of Europe have various political traditions. These
political traditions have, in their own way, been modified by
certain internally or externally imposed political systems which
have modified the social-cultural matrix of the society. Some of
these countries are uniquely parliamentary democracies; others
have tried and failed. Some struggle with greater or lesser success
in the area of democratic government. The communist
governments of eastern Europe are products as well as victims of
the unique military situation that developed in the aftermath of
World War II. Yet all are united in the concept of strengthening
the framework of society, and all are quite dedicated to the idea
that an individual owes a duty to his nation-state. The nation-
state is perceived as an entity with its own attributes, with its own
history, its present and its future. It is perceived as having its own
unique character; and its achievements, glory and power reflect
and endow its citizens with prestige.

The voice of the people through the legislature makes the rules
and regulations. The constitution is really a system of rules which
is modified constantly by the pressure of parliamentary debate or,
in the totalitarian countries, by the party in power that assumes it
speaks for the people. There is a general acceptance that political
parties are ideological; they may have different ways and
methods, but their goals are the same — namely, to seek a system
of social justice which will reflect glory and power on the state
and provide justice for the individual.

If anything, all these countries in some way, form or shape base
their assumption on natural moral law. (1) It is assumed that
there is such a concept as truth and that the legal system attempts
to find it. Unfortunately, this concept of natural law is, at times,
perverted, as it was under the Nazis in Germany, to justify and
condone the most horrendous excesses and cruelties.

The United States is philosophically quite different, since it is
not a country or a nation-state, but rather a conglomeration of
units (independent states) which, for a common cause of welfare
and defense, have united and adopted a constitution which gives
and guarantees each citizen a certain definable freedom. This

constitution is the living document by which all things are weighed and either found wanting or approved, and it is based on the 18th century concept of natural law and an *a priori* attempt to settle all possible difficulties which may bedevil men in their relationships with each other.

Many commentators on American life have written that the aristocracy of America is the legal profession and that the Americans are enamored by law. (2) Decisions regarding the most mundane everyday affairs which affect the welfare of countless numbers of individuals are made by judges, not in the context of what is the majority decision or of what is in the best interests of the people involved, but in the context of the constitution. These decisions affect voting power, the bussing of children and the rights of criminals. Whereas in a European parliamentary system a vote of no confidence would have been sufficient to send the head of the government out of office and such a vote of no confidence could have been made on any real or imagined issue, in the United States the constitution protects a president from being displaced as much as it protects any individual citizen.

In the civilized world human affairs are managed and arranged by the legal system. It is the legal profession that administers the comprehensive system of laws regulating the everyday affairs of man, whether these be the making of a will, the buying of property, or the more complex situations dealing with tort actions or problems of family law. The attorney is involved in so many problems in such an intimate fashion that, in fact, it is the attorney and the priest only that have, in Anglo-Saxon law, an historical privilege of being able to keep their clients' confidence inviolate. This privilege in practice means that anything the attorney hears in the process of a professional relationship cannot be divulged even in the process of a trial. This is known as "privileged communication." The attorney is, as it were, an extension of his client.

The role of the judiciary in the United States has certain unique characteristics which make it different from those of other countries.

In most totalitarian states, the judiciary is very much an extension of the state, and thus acts to work towards achieving the reconciliation of bringing the disaffected individual back to full participation within the social system. The individual may, first of all, of course, have to pay a price to be rehabilitated, but it is done in "the interest" of promoting his future welfare as a citizen and towards showing him the error of his ways. This is not very different from the medieval inquisition. This philosophy underlies the system of all civil law countries, whose legal traditions stem from the Code Napoleon.

Most democratic countries, particularly of the English-speaking world, have an independent judiciary which, with greater or lesser success, attempts to seek the truth and to interpret the legal system within the guidelines laid by the elected body. The people make the rules by electing representatives to the legislature, the legislature passes on the rules and regulations and the judiciary administers them in that spirit.

The United States, however, is unique in that the country is not a nation-state, but a people with a constitution, and it is to the constitution that the oath of office of the President is taken and that people swear allegiance on becoming citizens. The high priests of that constitution are the judges of the Supreme Court, and their acolytes are the attorneys. Rather than attempting to resolve problems by a socially desirable verdict, in the United States problems are seen as issues to be decided in the context of the constitution. However, since the constitution was written nearly 200 years ago, it is the Supreme Court that makes its judgments as to what the facts are as, for example, deciding that life begins at twenty-six weeks of pregnancy!

The legal profession has, to a large extent, set up its own rules, set up its own system of rights and wrongs and is, without doubt, politically power hungry. All sociological problems are meant to fall within its bailiwick. Furthermore, there is a tremendous struggle within the professions which is unique to the United States. Osteopaths and regular physicians battle it out in courts for legitimacy. The legitimacy is often whether medical insurance covers osteopathic treatment in the same way it does regular medical treatment. Psychology, social work and psychiatry are deadlocked in claiming expertise in the treatment and diagnosis of psychosocial problems. The nursing profession wishes to establish its autonomy, and many of its organized groups are rebelling against the alleged authoritarianism and dominance of the medical profession.

This trouble is unique to the United States, but the legal profession is filling a vacuum left very much by the organized church. It is becoming a third estate, with monopoly over the judiciary and inordinate influence over the executive and legislature. It is the profession that interprets the constitution in the spirit of the current day's morality. This constitution is interpreted by judges who, obviously, are attorneys. No one reflects or finds it peculiar for a Supreme Court judge to preface his remarks that a certain situation is not in keeping with the spirit of the constitution. I cannot imagine any other country's judge making such a statement, since it would be completely incomprehensible and legal nonsense! It is either the law or it isn't, but what does the spirit of the constitution have to do with the legal system?

I posit that the legal profession wishes to claim exclusive control over all social and political aspects of life in the United States. Hence, in this area of social implication of medical practice — namely, involuntary hospitalization and the issues of informed consent stemming from it — the attorneys have challenged medicine and have extended their professional interest! This recapitulates to a considerable extent the struggle of the middle ages between the medical profession and the theologian. The words of DeTocqueville are prophetic:

> In visiting the Americans and studying their laws, we perceived that the authority they have entrusted to members of the legal profession, and the influence that these individuals exercise in the government, are the most powerful existing security against the excesses of democracy.

However, this is a double-edged sword in that this very concept of an independent judiciary has raised serious questions whether the United States is really a democracy. It is, indeed, a Republic, and it has, indeed, suffrage and an elected legislature. But the judiciary is so independent that it is not under the control of any group except of the legal profession. DeTocqueville writes further:

The members of the legal profession have taken part in all the movements of political society in Europe for the last 500 years. At one time they had been the instruments of the political authorities, and at another they have succeeded in converting the political authorities into their instruments. In the middle ages, they afforded a powerful support to the crown; and since that period they have exerted themselves effectively to limit the royal prerogative.

Further, DeTocqueville writes:

Some of the tastes and habits of the aristocracy may consequently be discovered in the characters of lawyers. They participate in the same instinctive love of order and a formality; and they entertain the same repugnance to the actions of the multitude, and the same secret contempt of the government of the people.

DeTocqueville gives advice which may be of utmost importance to the medical profession:

Lawyers are attached to public order beyond every other consideration, and the best security of public order is authority. It must not be forgotten, also, that if they prize freedom much, they generally value legality still more: they are less afraid of tyranny than of arbitrary power; and provided the legislature undertakes of itself to deprive men of their independence, they are not dissatisfied.

If the medical profession can in a sensible and pragmatic manner, while about its lawful business of treating the mentally ill, obtain cooperation of the legal profession, then my prediction is that much of the current acrimony will begin to abate.

However, it may very well be (and here I admit I get far afield of this particular monograph) that the medical profession may be forced to play the role of permanent and loyal opposition. It may be that the issue of the mentally ill is the place to stop the growing tyranny of law, just as the issue of insanity and psychiatry's pathetic failure to play a meaningful role marked the peak of its influence.

DeTocqueville, with an historical perspective, writes:

Five hundred hears ago the English nobles headed the people and spoke in their name; at the present time, the aristocracy supports the throne and defends the Royal prerogative. But notwithstanding this, the aristocracy has its peculiar instincts and propensities. We must be careful not to confound isolated members of a body with the body itself. In all free governments, of whatever form they may be, members of the legal profession will be found in the front ranks of all parties. The same remark is also applicable to the aristocracy; almost all the democratic movements that have agitated the world have been directed by nobles. A privileged body can never satisfy the ambition of all its members: it has always more talents and more passions than it can find places to employ, so that a considerable number of individuals are usually to be met with who are inclined to attack those very privileges which they cannot soon enough turn to their own account.

It is my contention that much of the agitation and the concern expressed at potential thought control that is directed at the medical profession and psychiatry, in particular, has to do with this very aspect of the legal profession's wishing to establish its own control over this very powerful social tool. The fact that this influence is no where near as strong as the attorney suspects does not, in any way, limit the possibilities of social and psychological coercion in the minds of many attorneys.

I do not accept the contention that the attorneys' arguments are anti-intellectual. I am convinced that they are practicing a time-honored legal tactic of emphasizing a particular point to its extreme to obtain significant advantage and to significantly affect a particular situation.

A saying has it that the "business of America is business." I would not imply that the pursuit of material wealth is any greater in this country than elsewhere or that venality is more prevalent here than in any other country in the world, but it is accepted, rightly or not, that the profession of medicine in the United States is more interested in making money and monopolizing its prerogatives than in serving mankind than is medicine elsewhere. Medicine, as well as other professions, is more than a professional occupation; it is, indeed, big business. Again, many commentators have remarked that the individual American may see in his own local family doctor a dedicated individual, but he sees the profession of medicine as self-serving, money-grabbing and socially unconcerned. Hence the great concern, unique to the United States, for accountability of the medical profession to insurance companies.

Europe has accepted the contention that certain forms of maladaptive behavior are symptomatic of a disease — namely, of mental illness — and that this lies within the competence of the medical profession to diagnose responsibly and treat appropriately. It is seen as a duty of society to take care of and to treat its sick and as a civic obligation of the sick to be so treated and restored to health. The medical profession does not expect to become rich from fulfilling such a social obligation, while society does not feel that they have to be treated as second-class citizens or exposed to second-class conditions. There is a trust in the profession to be ethical and an acceptance that these problems are medical and have to be treated and handled in a medical context. Psychiatric facilities are as much a part of the whole medical scheme as any other hospital, unlike the situation in the United States, where insurance is unwilling to reimburse for chronic psychiatric hospitalization and where continually and inevitably states, counties and the federal government all attempt to disclaim financial responsibility. (3)

I recognize that I have presented a rather caricatured picture of the differences, but I think it important to accentuate the differences so that the concerns reflected in the different statutes can be better understood. European civilization accepts the premise that the sick should be treated to bring them back to the mainstream of their community life. The profession of medicine is endowed with a sense of trust to implement what society mandates, and the legal profession's role is to administer the regulations so that the mandates are implemented. In the United States the concern has to do with individual liberties rather than state prerogatives, and the legal profession jealously guards the liberties of the citizen to prevent the intrusion of the powerful state into the everyday life of the citizen. There is no feeling of accomplishment from the power or the glory of the state and, in fact, it is seen by many as an evil which should, if possible, be torn down so that a more equitable society can be built in the future. Many attorneys refuse to accept the possibility that mental illness affects the exercise of free will. However, there are those who assume that it may, but feel that this is the price the citizens have to pay for the upholding of individual freedoms. (4) In fact, this is an ideological position which argues that the price that the individual citizen has to pay for his liberty is to take a chance on being sick and untreated. This is contrary to the understanding of natural law, but it is a definitive and conscientious interpretation of the "spirit" of the constitution. Article V in the amendment to the constitution passed in 1791 states, "No person shall be deprived of life, liberty or property without due process of law." The fact that this article deals with criminal issues does not prevent it from being argued as the operative factor determining the relationship of society to the mentally ill and the obligations of society to the mentally ill.

It is difficult to summarize the development of legal thinking in the area of concern about the rights of the mentally ill. The current interest of many attorneys in this area appears to be directly related to the heightened interest in the rights of minorities which have emerged in the 1950's. While the average individual tends to see the legal profession as dedicated to the pursuit of justice and truth, attorneys, more often than not, in moments of honesty, describe their role as the administrators of statutes and as the arbitrators of arguments. It has been said more in truth than in jest that the good attorney is the one who can arbitrate a situation without ever needing to go to court. Recently and strikingly, in the United States (more than in any other country), lawyers have become the advocates for policy and social change. The civil rights, particularly school integration and bussing are the best examples. This has led to comments that attorneys are merely politicians in black robes and, in fact, is well-documented in attempts to fill vital court vacancies with appropriate and acceptable political figures. (5) There is no hesitation in a liberal politician's demanding that places on the Supreme Court be given to those who espouse liberal, progressive (whatever those value judgments may mean) philosophies! It is well understood that the legal system in this country not only interprets the mores of society, but often is in the vanguard of social change and of policy making.

The attorney's professional concern and expertise in dealing with the mentally ill was traditionally either involved with the protection of the inherent freedom of the individual through the process of habeas corpus or with the protection of the property and family rights of society. These concerns had to deal with such issues as testamentary capacity in order to protect the inherent family structure from arbitrary and incompetent will-making of an elderly, senile patient. The dangerous, if they belonged to the "establishment," were always to some degree protected by an insistence that a physician be involved in the adjudication for the necessity of involuntary confinement; the poor were the passive victims of the local arbitrators of the poor. The dangerous were often thrown into jail, the harmless allowed to wander around or put in work houses and poor houses.

The current state of the profession in regard to the mentally ill can be perhaps best expressed as one of extreme naivete, exaggerated ideological concern mixed with complete and absolute disinterest.

However, legal authors summarize some of the philosophical purposes and standards behind the various legal statutes. These have to do with the police power of the state and with the *parens patriae* responsibility philosophy of the state. Summarized, the police power refers to the protection of the citizen from harm that may result from dangerous and erratic conduct on the part of some of its citizens and, in this case, those who are labeled as suffering from mental illness. The *parens patriae* protects individuals, society and particularly family members from emotional harm resulting from the activities, behavior and conduct of a family member suffering from mental illness. The law is also concerned with the protection of society, the family, property and financial interests from the irresponsible activities of those members of the community and of the family who are suffering from mental illness. (6)

It is the police powers of the state which have traditionally been applied to legally justify the incarceration and commitment of the mentally ill. However, even going back to antiquarian times, the state also exercised its *parens patriae* philosophy of protecting those who could not be protected and by caring for those who could not care for themselves. This philosophical duty was often delegated to local communities, to monasteries, religious orders and orphanages. There is evidence that throughout historical times communities have tended to display a certain compassion, however rude and however rough, for those who could not be taken care of, who could not take care of themselves. While now we may look with horror at the children sent down into the coal mines of England at age twelve or thirteen, even in those days orphans were not abandoned or left to starve, but were brought up according to the social and religious beliefs of that society. The mentally ill were also taken care of as wards of the state, and this situation and philosophy continues to exist to this day.

The state has slowly inflicted the value of universal literacy and education for all its citizens. Now all who can possibly profit from the educational system are required and expected under penalty of law to attend school till age fifteen or sixteen. This is one of the *parens patriae* aspects of our western civilization. Requirements for inoculations, annual physicals and health inspections, enforced in various ways (at some times more than others and by some communities more than by others) are all results of this philosophy. It was disparingly referred to as the birth of the therapeutic state when Judge Shaw stated that one of the indications for involuntary treatment of a mentally ill citizen is the need for psychiatric treatment. (7) This particular philosophy, somewhat poorly articulated and opposed by many attorneys, has now become one of the accepted legal traditions behind involuntary hospitalization. This is also one of the major bones of contention and one of the main sources of argument against this particular practice. Certainly, many of the current practices are unreasonable and probably harmful, as are many of the practices in the school systems. One can think of no better example of the scandalous approach to the educational and emotional needs of the urban youth than the school systems that proliferate in this country. However, the answer to that is not necessarily to either abolish education or all teachers, nor is it to deny the reality of the need for some kind of an educational process for the youngster. It seems to me that the same example holds true for many of the current problems in the area of the involuntary hospitalization of the mentally ill.

The medical profession is faced with concerns about its own scientific and professional future. The psychiatric profession is faced with the same conflicts of redefining its role and scope and is being challenged by psychology and social work. The legal profession, perhaps, has managed to keep its own discipline more intact and has fewer intruders on its territorial space. It is also, however, trying to work out within its own ranks a form of ethics, professional goals and standards which is compatible with the expectations of society and its own traditions. Its traditions speak of protecting the life of all citizens. Unfortunately, human behavior and relationships, which fall within the expertise of the psychiatrist, are also considered to be within the expertise of the attorney. It would seem rather unlikely that an attorney would use his judgment in the interpretation of the figures for calculating the construction of a bridge. He may call on an expert with more credentials, greater acclaim, or possibly more credibility in order to better represent his client. In the area of human contact, however, it is quite clear that the average attorney is convinced that his own judgment, his own expertise and his own professional background is sufficiently expert to enable him to make judgments on intra-psychic and interpersonal behavior. This is a trap and a problem which has no easy or clear-cut answers. Dealing with clients and with people, many attorneys *do* develop skills which reflect their inherent intuition and ability to grasp the various levels of motivation behind the conduct of their clients. Many attorneys are very skilled in pursuing reasoning and lines of questioning which elicit either confused or inchoate thinking of the examinee. Many have taken psychology and sociology courses which have exposed them to certain levels of thinking in the area of the social sciences. (8) Some have experienced psychological difficulties themselves, particularly those who have attended the more prestigious institutions where college mental health services are readily available, and have actually availed themselves of psychiatric counselling and help. Often, this has led to their own perceptions that society would regard them as mentally ill and potentially fit subjects for confinement.

If this be true, which I think it is not, then it is understandable that they might feel a certain resentment and even potentially a certain feeling of paranoia. They abstract from this and, I think, overidentify with some of society's more unfortunate and disabled people. Lovers of freedom themselves, able to function autonomously, driven by their own internal strivings for professional success, they find it difficult to understand that much of society is composed of people who are barely able to function and who need constant gratification and dependency fulfillment for day-to-day survival. The "institutionalized" syndrome is found outside of asylums as well.

Again, in the United States where the term "character" has become merely a psychiatric expression for personality behavior, many of the attorneys express the egalitarian conviction of the American democracy that all have been created equal and that everyone has inherently the same quantity of character strength and will power.

Ultimately, the issue of how society approaches and develops its relationship to those who are mentally ill and who are currently being hospitalized, albeit involuntarily, will develop not so much on the expertise and success of the medical profession in developing treatments and standards for diagnoses as it will on the legal profession's own perception of the problem, its ideological commitment and its ability to feel that it has, within its own power, the ability to both practice a *parens patriae* philosophy and to protect the inherent freedoms and rights of the individual. In fact, it would seem that as psychiatry and the medical profession become more clearcut in their diagnostic ability and more able to apply and predict outcomes, then more social and ideological problems will be raised, and the issue of the therapeutic state will become a dilemma which needs to be resolved by social process. It will become both a greater threat as well as a greater temptation.

In addition to this concern is the current collusion of financially concerned and embarrassed states and their legislatures who are faced by a tax-payers' revolt. While in Europe the mentally ill are treated in hospitals budgeted through the medical payments, in this country all the state facilities are paid for by a variety of contributions from counties or state governments. This financial concern contributes to an attitude which makes it more difficult for patients to be hospitalized, for discouraging involuntary admissions and for making the criteria for emergency and involuntary commitment more restrictive. The recent successful law suits arguing the rights of the mentally ill to treatment have probably, if anything, tended to accentuate this trend. There is one other reason which explains many of the differences and which goes to the heart of the concern in the United States about involuntary commitment, and that has to do with the racial, religious and ethnic minorities and their growing awareness of their own identities.

Most European countries are quite homogeneous and have well-established social-economic class systems. Those countries which have more than one nationality, e.g. the United Kingdom, still have historical and traditional separation. The Scots tend to live in Scotland where they form the working class, the middle class and the aristocracy, and, by and large, the English tend to live in England where they also tend to form the spectrum of society. The English docker or the Polish coal miner may, in their own class consciousness, rage at class exploitation, but they share the same tradition and are moved by the same goals of material comfort and profess the same goals of social equity and strive for the same manners as their middle classes. Their concern may be that the treatment for illness is not available to the lower class or that the beds are not as comfortable, but there is no inherent fear that the value systems will be compromised. The United States, in comparison, is made up of countless groups of divergent racial, religious and ethnic backgrounds. The middle class is basically just one generation old. The minority groups are all looking for an identity, and the middle class has little established historical perspective. The competition between the various groups for a position on the socioeconomic ladder is bitter and is reflected, for example, in the current explosion of numbers of applicants to medical and law schools. Psychiatric treatment is perceived in a very ambivalent fashion. On one hand it is considered a socially desirable and worthwhile therapeutic interaction which should be available to all on an equitable basis; on the other hand, it is seen as potentially dangerous behavior modification which may impair, challenge or inhibit the rightful expression of a minority group's identity aspirations.

I well recall the days when patients refused or were embarrassed to talk about their religious or sexual attitudes and practices. Now among the young the same holds true for their political and social concerns. They will, with great comfort, discuss their life-styles and eagerly await interpretations of their feelings about their spouses or their parents. But if a mention is made that some of their rebelliousness or civil rights dedication is a reflection of unconscious conflict, more often than not treatment is unilaterally terminated as they stalk off in a huff. Many of the minority groups react to psychiatry in a similar fashion. They would like it, but want to control it and want to be safe within it. Hence, the cry for black psychiatrists for the blacks, for women therapists who will not be hung up by Freudian analytic theories and so on and so forth.

In such a situation, involuntary treatment and commitment becomes a further and more potent threat, since it exposes the individual to value systems of a feared and alien profession, no longer of a trusted one. It exposes the patient to value systems with which the individual may not identify, unlike the European patient who, by and large, looks up to the academic and scholarly success achieved in the person of his physician. There is a mixture of concern both at the challenge to the belief as well as the fear of not being understood.

In my judgment, these are some of the reasons that have, over the years, led to the variety of practices and the differences as well as bitter acrimony over the approaches to the mentally ill between the United States and the rest of the world. Since it is quite evident that this is a reflection of current political and social problems, then it is a situation which is most unlikely to change and, in fact, one might predict that there may be an eruption of similar concerns in those countries of Europe where new migrant groups have established themselves in the last thirty years.

NOTES

1. Black's Law Dictionary defines natural law, as, JUS NATURALE. The

natural law, or law of nature; law or legal principles, supposed to be discoverable by the light of nature or abstract reasoning, or to be taught by nature to all nations and men alike; or law supposed to govern men and people in a state of nature, i.e. in advance of organized governments or enacted laws." This concept originated with the philosophical jurists of Rome, and was gradually extended until the phrase came to denote a supposed basis or substratum common to all system of positive law, and hence to be found, in greater or lesser purity, in the laws of all nations. And, conversely, they held that if any rule or principle of law was observed in common by all peoples with whose systems they were acquainted, it must be a part of the jus naturale, or derived from it. Thus the phrases "jus naturale" and "just gentium" came to be used interchangeably.

2. I am referring here specifically to the writings of Alexis DeTocqueville and his classic description of the early American federal period, *Democracy in America*, 9th ed. *(New York, Alfred A. Knopf, 1963).*

3. The American Psychiatric Society continues to wage a rather uphill battle in trying to obtain comprehensive insurance for psychiatric illness. It has obtained somewhat half-hearted, minimal support of its constituent individual members. As of 1974, few of the insurance companies provide such coverage with the exception of the federal Blue Cross and some of the major medical catastrophic insurance programs. Neither of the two highly touted national health insurance schemes give anywhere near the necessary insurance for psychiatric disability and illness. The states (even some of the more advanced ones in the northeast) have taken a position that they are not in the business of providing medical care to their population and that their job is only to provide the most rudimentary services to those who are unable to fend for themselves . . . very much a variation of the work house.

4. The American Civil Liberties Union Memo #1, December, 1969, of the City of New York takes a very ideological position on this issue. It states, "Proponents of civil confinement of the mentally ill quite correctly argue that abolition of involuntary confinement would cause much human degradation and social harm, but less, perhaps, than its retention." There is no denial here of the tragedies and inference that certain evils are preferable to others.

5. For example, during the Nixon appointments to the Supreme Court, there was a great concern that the traditional Jewish seat on the Supreme Court of the United States be retained. There are frequent nominations of politicians to high judicial responsibility at times, counter to any first-hand judicial experience of the individual in question. The example that springs to mind is the ex-Governor of the State of Illinois, Otto Kerner.

6. *Harvard Law Review*, "Civil Commitments of the Mentally ill: Theories and

Procedures." An editorial 79:1288-1298 (1966), and R. H. Chused, "Due process for all constitutional standards for involuntary civil sommitment and release," *University of Chicago Law Review,* 34:633-660 (1967). J. M. Livermore, C. P. Malmquist, and P. E. Meehl, "On the justification for civil commitment." *University of Pennsylvania Law Review,* 117:75-96 (1968).

7. A. Deutxch, *The Mentally Ill in America* (Nee York, Columbia University Press, 1949).

8. It has been commented that at the undergraduate college level, courses in sociology and psychology are taught by young, often quite radical faculty, who are very venomous in their condemnation of society in general and medicine in particular.

CHAPTER VI

COMPARISON STUDIES

$\mathbf{A}$ REVIEW of literature shows a paucity of comparison studies on involuntary hospitalization and commitment of the mentally ill. The World Health Organization gave a report on the subject in 1955, but has so far not done any comparative studies. (1) Part of this is probably understandable in that the statutory language does not necessarily imply an understanding of the practices. It is well known that even in small states like Connecticut, practices tend to vary from community to community even though the statutory language is uniform.

The Bar Association of New York wrote a very authoritative study from a legal perspective of the problems of the involuntarily committed citizen and, as part of this study, a brief comparative review of some European studies was included. (2) As part of the study by Peszke and Wintrob which was reported in the *American Journal of Psychiatry,* a library search of the rules pertaining to commitment of a number of English-speaking countries was done. (3) The questionnaire was sent out to a number of European, South American and Asian countries. My colleague, Dr. Ronald Wintrob, psychiatrist and anthropologist, also gave valuable information from his experience in some of the African countries where he had worked as part of the cultural psychiatry programs. (4)

It has to be emphasized that it is difficult, if not impossible, to interpret the practice that is followed by physicians from merely reading statutes, since it is the pragmatic implementation that is really important and not necessarily the statutory language. The most rigorously written regulations and built-in checks will have little if no effect if the individual physician, attorney and judge are, at best, only marginally interested in the problem or unaware of the problems of the mentally ill. On the other hand, commitment procedures which leave the implementation solely to medical judgment and which, on reading, appear to leave a great deal to the medical judgment of the physician may, in fact, be quite equitable if the professional judgment and ethics of the profession are of the highest order.

Poland, for example, under its current statutes, leaves this judgment of involuntary hospitalization solely to the discretion of a physician who refers such a patient to the hospital and to the staff psychiatrist who decides to admit him. (5) However, the physician and psychiatrist are both expected to state *extensively* their observations and indications for making a conclusion that the patient needs to be hospitalized. It is rather interesting that the staff psychiatrist *may* refuse to admit such a patient if he is not convinced on the basis of his examination that such admission is necessary. However, it is interesting that refusal of admission for lack of room is not justified!

When I discussed the commitment practices in Poland with some of the psychiatrists and questioned the problem of possible infringement of civil rights, my comments were met with some degree of amusement. I was shown a facility which indeed was superior to the majority of British or American state psychiatric institutes and which was undoubtedly superior to the average Polish citizen's own apartment. The psychiatrist explained that they are continually caught by shortages of beds and have to discharge patients prematurely. However, if a patient feels aggrieved at involuntary confinement, he can ask the local district attorney (procurator) to investigate. I was also told that a suit had successfully been brought against a referring physician and admitting psychiatrist and that punitive damages had been assessed for a technical irregularity.

The situation in Austria reveals that there a forensic legal psychiatrist is used to evaluate the patient's need for involuntary commitment. This seems to be somewhat typical of the Germanic academic tradition of using skilled expertise in the decision-making process, an appoach quite different from the dilettante approach of the British and American societies.

The English and Welsh system is different from the Scottish one, since the first allows two physicians to involuntarily commit a patient to a psychiatric institution. The Scottish system, however, mandates that two physicians recommend such a procedure to a sheriff (in Scotland, an attorney) who then makes a legal order for such a commitment. Respondents from both systems praised the merits and progressive features of their respective regulations. The English system was praised as a strictly medical one in which the patient is protected from having his confidences and his problems made known to individuals who will not be involved in his treatment. The Scottish psychiatrists felt strongly that their system was better in that the patient could not be insulted or prejudiced against his doctors by thinking that they had initiated commitment and would "blame" the sheriff. Furthermore, the opinion was that the legal properties were better protected in the Scottish system.

Both countries have an automatic review system — namely, the Mental Health Tribunal. (6)

It seems that the issue is quite well focused here in the difference between England and Wales on one hand and in Scotland on the other — namely, the degree and the level of trust that is present in society and the order of priorities that society sees at its particular stage of development.

In the undeveloped countries, lack of facilities and lack of professional expertise leads to the neglect or the ignoring of this question. In the past, the British Isles and the Colonies dealt with the dangerous, such as paupers and the insane, by sending them to jail. Within the United States itself there is a fantastic difference which has been well discussed by a number of authors. (7) This diversity of approach to the problem has not been, as far as my own research is concerned, sufficiently analyzed in the English literature. Yet the differences are like day and night and, even in countries sharing similar medical syyems, these approaches tend to vary; e.g. while Scotland and England appear to have comparable systems, another country with a similar medical educational philosophy, Ireland, has a significantly different approach. Apart from the different requirements for the implementation, the definition of individuals who may be fit subjects for confinement also tends to vary considerably.

It would seem that the problem of involuntary commitment of the mentally ill is not a medical imperative in the same way as is the excision of an appendix. The diagnosis of mental illness is more of a cultural phenomenon and is affected by a variety of practices and theories as well as by the social development of the given society. Stigma of hospitalization for mental illness is strong and in some countries quite biased. Some jurisdictions will automatically withdraw the medical license of a committed physician. Senator Eagleton in 1972, on the basis of his own psychiatric history, was deprived of the opportunity of running as a vice-presidential candidate.

In Chapter I, I have presented an outline of the historical vicissitudes of society in relation to the mentally ill. The current differences between philosophy and practice reflect and mirror the current political, social and cultural developments of many societies. In many of the so-called underdeveloped countries where western medicine and the western legal system is but a patina over indigenous practices, the mentally ill are still treated in a manner in no way different from the practice of the American colonies in the 18th century. In the research study a number of South and Central American correspondents confirmed that involuntary hospitalization practices as late as 1972 illustrated the trust of society in the medical profession and their fear of legal intervention and involvement. (8) This, of course, is coupled with the existence of many archaic laws which equate involuntary hospitalization with insanity and lack of competency.

There are two conclusions to be made from looking at the problem in other countries. The variety of legal, medical and social remedies which exist are directly related to the complexity of the problem.

Any profession or any individual who claims to have simple or easyunswers is fooling himself and his audience or readers. Inevitably in countries of the Western World as their traditional social patterns become modified, the issue is most likely to surface.

Secondly, this aspect should be studied by an international, interdisciplinary body. The World Health Organization has the best possible opportunity to recruit reputable lawyers, psychiatrists, sociologists and political scientists to study the implications of the problem and to present facts as opposed to theories, traditional practices and ideologies.

NOTES

1. World Health Organization Technical Report 98, 155. "Legislation affecting psychiatric treatment," Geneva, July, 1955. This specific report had the following conclusionary statement:

> What is required is to give these patients facilities for treatment and the possibility of guardianship and medical supervision in accordance with their medical needs and social inadequacy. The different methods of solving these problems are extremely complex since they must vary according to the social structure of each country. No one system can be applicable to several different countries and even in one and the same country the systems advocated by some will be repudiated by others. Any system which comes into conflict with legal or cultural conceptions is inapplicable. It would seem, therefore, that preference should be given above all to establishing laws strongly integrated into cultural traditions while at the same time leaving the way open for possible changes.

The Royal Commission on the Law Relating to Mental Illness and Mental Deficiency, Report 19, 1954-1957, Her Majesty's Stationery Office, 1957 stated,

> We recommend that the law should be altered so that whenever possible suitable care may be provided for mentally disordered patients with no more restriction of liberty or legal formality than is applied to people who need care because of other types of illness, disability or social difficulty. Compulsory power should be used in future only when they are positively necessary to override the patient's own unwillingness or the unwillingness of his relatives, for the patient's own welfare or for the protection of others.
>
> When compulsion has to be used, there must be special procedures and safeguards. We recommend new procedures for this purpose which would replace the present certification procedures. We hope that the term 'certification' and the ideas associated with it will fall completely into disuse and that the public will recognize that these procedures carry no implications about the probable length or cause of the patient's illness or disability.

For a discussion of some of this, see Reports of Committees — Royal Commission on the Law Relating to Mental Illness and Mental Deficiency discussed by N. Morris, *Modern Law Review*, 21:63-68 (1958).

2. Association of the Bar of the City of New York. *Mental Illness and Due Process*. (New York, Cornell University Press, 1962).

3. This study was supported by the University of Connecticut Research Foundation Grant No. 5172-36-30110-35-012. John Burns, Esq., a member of the Connecticut Bar did the library research. Some of the conclusions of the study were reported by M. A. Peszke, and R. M. Wintrob, "Emergency Commitment — A Transcultural Study," *American Journal of Psychiatry*, 131:36-40 (1974).

4. See Supra footnote #3. Also R. M. Wintrob, and E. D. Wittkower, "Witchcraft in Liberia and its psychiatric implications" in S. Lesse, ed., *An Evaluation of the Results of Psychotherapies*. (Springfield, Charles C Thomas, 1968).

5. The regulation is an executive order of the Polish Minister of Health promulgated as Instruction 120-52. Decided on the 10th of December, 1952 and published in the official newsletter of the Ministry of Health, taking immediate effect on the 15th of December, 1952. This is an executive order emanating from a Minister of Health pertaining to involuntary psychiatric hospitalizations. While one assumes that at some level this was discussed and possibly approved by appropriate legislative (or party) authorities, the strength of the practice is based on a purely medical directive.

6. J. C. Wood, "Mental Health Review Tribunals," *Medical Science & Law*, 7:86-92 (1971).

7. H. A. Davidson, "The Commitment Procedures and their Legal Implications" in S] Arieti, *American Handbook of Psychiatry*. (New York, Basic books, 1959). The late Dr. Davidson, internationally known forensic psychiatrist, showed great scholarliness and wit in preparing the chapter on commitments; e.g. he writes,

> Most North American psychiatrist would indeed be delighted if the proverb 'As Maine goes, so goes the nation' could apply to commitment papers. The medical certificate in a Maine commitment paper simply requires a statement that the patient is insane.

He analyzes the different procedures in all the states and, while conceivably this may not be up to date, it shows the variety of procedures. In the State of Washington, for example, he (the physician) has to fill out four full pages and also swear that "This is not a case of harmless, chronic mental unsoundness." In this report Dr. Davidson comments that some states expect the physician to comment on whether the patient has burial insurance; some demand to know his criminal record. A number require a comment about the patient's literacy and some require the patient's social security number. One state, at that point, required the patient's draft classification and Mississippi, in 1959, at least, wished to know whether the marriage was happy, while Newfoundland expects the physician to alert the hospital whether any of his (the patient's) children are illigitimate.

For more up-to-date and more legalistic approach without the flavor of Davidson's work, see the comprehensive S. J. Brakel, and R. S. Rock, ed; *The mentally disabled and the law*. (Chicago University, Chicago Press, 1971). Also, M. Birnbaum, "Some comments on the right to treatment," *Archives of General Psychiatry*, 13:34-45, (1965), discusses the epidemiology of commitment and shows the variation in the United States. The table which is appended in the article and which is based on statistical data prepared by the Mental Health Statistics of the National Institute of Mental Health for 1962 and published in 1963 shows that there were 1767 committed resident inmates per hundred thousand general population in Washington, D.C.; 517.5 per hundred thousand in New York and as little as 91.6 per hundred thousand in Utah. How much of this has to do with the different commitment procedures and how much of it has to do with the degree of urbanization of the different states is rather difficult to establish.

8. See Supra footnote #3; M. A. Peszke, and R. M. Wintrob, "Emergency Commitment — A Transcultural Study." In that research, we obtained a number of direct quotes from some physicians and the following was quite illuminating:

> We very rarely have to commit patients. The poor people, without relatives, are taken directly to the state hospital and held there until they get better, even if they claim that they did not enter as a voluntary patient. Even rich patients are held in private hospitals until they recover enough or threaten a legal action if they are not released. Rarely we have to go to court to commit a patient. We don't have much problem in this respect since the poor are usually, if at all, committed to the mental hospitals. The closest relative usually makes the patient accept hospitalization. I would leave it the way it is now, otherwise private hospitals may be very much afraid of hospitalizing a patient without his signature or that of the closest relative!

CHAPTER VII

SUGGESTIONS FOR THE FUTURE

AFTER having reviewed the historical perspective and the evolution of the asylum from a custodial institution to the far from fully implemented therapeutic hospital, and after having reviewed the current concepts of mental illness, the procedures for involuntary hospitalization in other countries and the current climate of concern, it is incumbent to synthesize and come up with suggestions. It is also obvious that suggestions are at times theoretical and need to be modified by experience as well as by realistic parameters of budgetary and staffing availability. Suggestions are outlines for implementation and for achievement of certain goals, but within these goals certain problems are more crucial and more pressing, and differing societies will have differing priorities. (1) The priorities are, to some extent, determined by the greatest perceived need and, to a lesser but still significant extent, affected by the availability of resources and the readiness with which these goals can be met.

One of the most perplexing facts confronting any practicing psychiatrist is the variety of statutes and regulations pertaining to commitment in the United States. Within this spectrum are requisites which range from the most archaic to the most legalistic, and the most socially progressive. Some meet the requirements that have been specified in the model draft Act and which were so well articulated by Isaac Ray over a hundred years ago. (2)

Ray's original comments to the psychiatrist have become as significant as have the words of John Stuart Mill to the advocate of civil liberties. Ray stated,

> In the first place the law should put no hindrance in the way to the prompt use of those instrumentalities which are regarded as most effectual in promoting the comfort and restoration of the patient. Secondly, it should spare all the necessary exposure of

private troubles and all unnecessary conflict with popular
prejudices. Thirdly, it should protect individuals from
wrongful imprisonment. It would be objection enough to any
legal provision that it failed to secure these objects in the
completest possible manner. (3)

The model draft Act attempted to deal with a number of these
issues and, indeed, many states have followed it to a larger or
smaller extent. It is perhaps New York State in this country and
the United Kingdom that have approached Ray's original
injunctions and the spirit of concern most closely. (4)

The implementation of managing this social and medical
problem depends on an understanding of what needs to be done,
its social and economic context and also on having facilities and
staff which are able to provide what society mandates and what
the medical and legal profession agree is ethically reasonable,
therapeutically useful and legally justified.

As long as society turns to physicians and to the medical setting
for help and for relief in those conditions that we refer to as
mental illness, it will be up to the medical profession to formulate
and to actively promote those interventions and procedures
which are ethical and in which the profession has a *competence*.
There are two resulting conclusions from this statement which
the medical profession has so far been derelict in admitting and in
bringing to the attention of society. Not all personality or even
psychological problems are treatable, and certainly many of the
problems of living fall just as readily into the lap of the
sociologist or the priest as they do into that of the physician.
These are the socioeconomic problems which rightfully belong to
the human resources aspect of social agencies. Like education,
rehabilitation may be strengthened by psychiatric knowledge and
input, but it is not psychiatric practice.

Yet in those areas which fall within the domain of the medical
profession and which can be diagnosed and in most instances
treated, in which the problem is not a long-standing personality
deviation but manifest by an onset of dystonic behavior,
psychological crisis and maladaptive regression, then psychiatry
as representative of the medical discipline is able to play its
traditional role of being a helping and treating profession. (5) I

think it imperative that medicine take a strong stand as a profession and articulate that medical criteria and medical judgments can only be *supplemented* by other professional inputs (such as from the law or social work), but that they cannot be circumvented or actively influenced by other professions. Medical treatment is subject to medical licensure, to tort action and peer review, but under no circumstance can medicine abrogate its primary responsibility. Neither should it "fudge" its actions, once society has changed the ground rules for its decision-making process.

If, indeed, as has been articulated by many attorneys, the legal profession has an inherent constitutionally given right to protect the freedom of citizens and this right gives them a "first crack" at a patient, then, indeed, in those jurisdictions the medical profession should leave the emergency room and psychiatric problem to the attorney. But society should be aware that it is the attorney who is staffing the emergency room! Furthermore, the medical profession should be better educated as to the statutes which regulate its competence and responsibility towards the mentally ill and should under no circumstance go beyond the criteria outlined by the legislature. The best interest of the patient does not in any way legally or ethically entitle the physician to "fudge" his assessment, nor, indeed, does the physician do society or his patient a favor by doing so. If the legislatures wish to have "tough" commitment laws, then that is society's wish articulated through its legislature. Society will have to live with this until it does change its rules. If indeed no great harm results from this as has been argued by many, then society will have gained a benefit; if harm to society results, then hopefully society will again listen to the medical profession. Perhaps both the medical and the legal professions will have the courage to look at this objectively and compare the different states and resulting differences.

Recently, the state of Connecticut, among many, changed its laws, emphasizing dangerousness as a criterion for emergency commitment. There is no evidence that I can find that the number of patients committed has markedly decreased as a result of the different language of the statutes. Yet the language emphasizes dangerousness, an area in which psychiatrists, indeed, have poor predictive ability. (6) I am not sure that anyone else has better knowledge in assessing individual potential for future dangerousness, but that is not the issue. If we understand dangerousness in its legal sense and in the sense that it is commonly used, then very few patients will be or can be committed. If, however, decisions regarding commitment are to be made by physicians, they ought to be made for the patient's welfare. No other reason is within the ethical province of the medical profession. And the criteria for intervention should be a therapeutic one of *restoring* the health of the individual; the drastic intervention of involuntary hospitalization should be done on behalf of the patient for his welfare, the protection of his property and of his family.

In those jurisdictions in which dangerousness is invoked as the only criterion, then society might as well employ sociologists, statisticians and attorneys to make predictions, and there is no reason for psychiatrists or physicians to intervene.

It is paradoxical, however, that the legal profession has had the opportunity over many centuries to influence and modify the criminal law process and the system of corrections and, as we all know, has failed dismally. Crime rates have skyrocketed; the correctional system in the words of all is "a public disgrace" which only tends to teach ineffectual criminals greater skills. We have seen recidivism increase. Why society would want the mentally ill and the psychiatric institutions to become exposed to this track record is perplexing, yet, indeed, commitment laws as they are being written and as they are interpreted by the attorneys, make it quite clear that psychiatrists have progressively less role in their implementation.

There is an indictment here of the medical profession in that it has failed because of its passivity and perhaps a certain amount of ineffectuality in conveying to society and to its elected representatives reasonable criteria for involuntary hospitalization. Too often society is blasted with statements that only two kinds of people get locked up: the criminals who have transgressed society's laws and the mentally ill who have transgressed psychiatry's laws. Such polemics, so easily refuted, have, however, been allowed to stand unchallenged.

There are cultural reasons in the United States which contribute to this problem — namely, the opportunity of many Americans to visit psychiatrists for psychotherapeutic intervention and the frequency with which they do so. Very often such contacts are frustrating, and the patient abandons his treatment with a sense of dissatisfaction and anger towards the psychiatrist. Whether these frustrations are neurotic or realistic is immaterial. The fact is that many have experienced frustrating psychotherapeutic contacts, and many, indeed, have been exposed to bad psychotherapists (or at least bad for their specific problem). Therefore, commitment is all too readily seen by many as a stock response on the part of physicians and psychiatrists in order to deal with any personality deviation or neurotic problem which may be written up or mentioned in any standard textbook of psychiatry.

In addition to the individual experience of a considerable number of Americans who have experienced some form of encounter group, counselling or psychotherapy, there is a rather unique American Attitude towards the mental health profession and its expertise. In Europe, the psychiatrist is regarded as a physician treating the "insane." While some practice psychoanalytic therapy and while office ambulatory practice is not exactly unknown, it does not enjoy the popularity or one could say the "fadism" that is enjoyed by psychiatrists, social workers and psychologists in the United States.

Society, furthermore, does not endow and the profession has not claimed to possess an expertise outside of the one-to-one patient/physician contact. Perhaps psychiatry and psychology have not flowered or matured in Europe as much as they have in the United States, and it is even possible that their full knowledge and sophistication have not been accepted as readily in Europe as in America, but it is a fact that for the average European, psychiatrists have no more expertise in determining the future of mankind or in correcting social problems than has the orthopedic surgeon or the dentist. In the United States, with its greater emphasis on social and environmental factors as determinants for behavior — an approach which has led to a completely anti-intellectual and anti-scientific denial of all biological and physiological factors as explanations for personality — people have turned to these social sciences both with hope and trepidation. An educated European fears and looks to psychiatry as little as he does to organized religion. In the United States, this existential vacuum becomes filled by the mental health movement, and that, indeed, begins to threaten the very autonomy of the individual. One does not fear philosophies or knowledge if one does not endow them with irrational power. Since the majority of us have some personality quirks or idiosyncracies and many of us have major neurotic problems which affect our professional, interpersonal or sexual lives, such construction of criteria for commitment leads to understandable concern. John Stuart Mill stated,

> The only purpose for which power can be rightfully exercised
> over any member of a civilized community, against his will, is to
> prevent harm to others. His own good, either physical or moral,
> is not a sufficient warrant.

Such is the basic philosophy behind the curtailment of involuntary hospitalization exclusively to problems of dangerousness. The contention of psychiatry (See Chap. III) is that the mentally ill individual lacks the ability to exercise his will and that abandoning him is to allow the despotism of mental illness to coerce and to prevent the inherent rightful and morally guaranteed pursuit of his own autonomy. Psychiatry as a profession has been derelict in making this point clear to society.

However, It is also true that medicine can only function in the cultural context of the given day and age and, while it should actively seek to educate the community and influence the legislature, it should be done in a way which does not leave it open to the challenge, however irrational, that it is merely trying to protect its "turf" or to enhance its own social power.

At the same time, once society *has* decided that criteria for commitment are such that psychiatry has no inherent professional expertise in meeting them, it should retire to the background. In such a setting, the attorney is the one who should staff the emergency room and make dispositions and judgments as to dangerousness.

The above suggestions may seem a little bit like "little Johnny" refusing to play with his friends if he cannot have his way. Yet I make that suggestion with the deepest conviction and seriousness. And I have effected, in my own practice, just that philosophy. However, it is also incumbent to come up with positive suggestions.

Let me break them down into two sections, one dealing with the practices for intervention and one dealing with suggestions for improvement in the treatment of people who fall within the system.

Emergency Detention

The emergency room of any hospital is now confronted by a large number of psychological and social problems. Many have to do with psychiatric problems such as acute schizrenia or problems due to the toxic effects of various drugs. Contrary to what society inherently believes and contrary to the impression learned by students from reading textbooks, diagnoses are rarely made on one examination. The majority of diagnoses in serious and even mild cases are made over a period of time. There has to be a situation in which these problems can be observed and evaluated. Patients should not be "sent" to some distant state psychiatric facility, but should, indeed, be observed by a skilled staff and, in a small number of cases, detained against their will until a judgment is made as to the etiology of the process and until such a time as an intelligent estimate of family resources and background and a treatment plan can be formulated. Such an emergency detention should be in a general hospital with significant input from internists and neurologists. It should have input from a social worker who can make an evaluation of the family strengths and contact appropriate family members or friends. Such emergency detention should have certain legal aspects in that the physician in charge of the emergency room should make a certificate outlining the reason why it is felt necessary for the patient's welfare for detention to be mandated. Under no circumstance should such a detention be longer than forty-eight hours, i.e. two working days.

There is every social advantage in having legal input to the situation or patient at this point. Some patients and families may need to be advised of the legal consequences that have precipitated or evolved from the illness. This may be particularly true for those who would wish to pursue treatment but are concerned about the financial costs. It may be true for the elderly who are unaware of how to manage their pensions or who, indeed, may need to have some kind of conservatorship initiated. It is vitally important, at this stage, to make a quick but accurate assessment of the stresses which have led to the patient's being brought to the emergency room and which have led to his maladaptive regression. It is, however, primarily a medical matter, and it should not be seen by the attorney as a field for the exercise of adversary proceeding, the bad guy being the physician and the good guy the attorney, the protector of freedom. The legal role should be circumscribed to the role of advising the physician as to some of the legal and social problems, to working with the family and, if in the attorney's judgment social transgressions have occurred, to alert either the public prosecutor or the Legal Aid Clinic to initiate a habeas corpus proceeding.

The attorney should be part of the investigative and therapeutic team at this stage of the proceeding. This is a role which many attorneys claim is ambiguous and, indeed, if it is so ethically uncomfortable, then they are better out of it completely, rather than participating in a context of which they have no comprehension and in which they can only be destructive to the patient.

This period of time should be seen as observational and diagnostic with an attempt to work out a treatment program if that is necessary. If any treatment is undertaken, it should be in the same philosophy as the use of analgesics for severe pain or antibiotics for infection. Antipsychotic medications which are safe and effective could fall within this philosophy. Any time during these forty-eight hours the emergency room physicians could request a local mental health tribunal for the initiation of involuntary hospitalization. In practice, we know from our own clinical experience that a very significant majority of patients at this point will either decide to admit themselves on a voluntary basis to a psychiatric institution or will have regained sufficient psychological adaptiveness to resume some kind of reasonably normal life within the context of their family. The greatest number of patients who are committed originate from settings such as emergency rooms of city hospitals where there is no flexibility for observation or psychosocial assessment and where family or social "lifelines" are nonexistent.

It is at the next step that significant and vital legal input is required, where it should be welcomed and where it serves the best interests of both society and physicians. On the basis of findings in the detention phase within the emergency room, a report should be submitted to the mental health tribunal. Reasonable counsel to the patient and the family should be obligatory. The attorney has a significant role at this point in examining all the evidence and in helping the psychiatrist clarify his thinking and elaborate his facts. Again, I emphasize that the psychiatrist should not advocate commitment but work towards a resolution in the best interests of the patient. Recommendations should only be made in the same context as recommendations by a physician for any kind of medical treatment. Under no circumstance should the psychiatrist ever become an advocate for the process of commitment, any more than he would advocate any course of treatment.

I would not see anything remiss in a significant number of such cases being adjudicated with a recommendation that no further inpatient treatment is required. Such a neutral body with such a nonpartisan position on the part of the physicians would be a protection to both the patient and the emergency room staff. Should anything ensue to the patient or the community (as suicide or perhaps something even more tragic such as a multiple murder), then the responsibility would be more fairly and evenly divided. Neither should this process be seen as an automatic referral in which every case seen and detained is automatically "bumped" to the tribunal for final opinion and adjudication to "free" the emergency room staff from making decisions. Peer review and continued education are important!

I have read with interest that some communities have begun to use mobile crisis intervention teams to visit the families' homes. There is no reason to discount the very beneficial and therapeutic aspect of such teams, and should commitment be necessary such a team should, and could, make a direct referral to the mental health tribunal with recommendations based on their fact finding.

Furthermore, at times, police officers or other welfare agencies need to apprehend individuals (while about their lawful business) who have shown sufficient evidence of mental illness and dangerousness. In those cases a direct application to the tribunal circumventing the observational period seems reasonable. In such a situation the role of the attorney will and should be more traditional and more protective of the patient's liberties than would be the case in the emergency room setting.

I am sure that, given the state of the art and the intense interest in experimenting with community programs such as crisis intervention teams, there will be a constant churning of ideas and creation of social, therapeutic models, some implemented and others falling by the wayside. It is also inevitable that even in any one state, let alone different geopolitical regions, some communities will be more advanced and progressive in relation to the creation of such outreach community programs. But the "mutual" protection of the detention period and of the tribunal seems a reasonable, uniform ideal that can be meaningfully attained by all communities.

There should, in fact, be one other route to the tribunal — one that is currently vested with great difficulties and, for many individuals, presents imponderable problems. This is an application on the part of a family for the confinement of one of their members as a result of mental illness or incompetency. Such situations develop most often with young schizophrenics or the elderly, when the onset is insidious over a period of time and certainly not dramatic or acute. Very often treatment by the family physician or by a combination of family physicians and practicing psychiatrists has demonstrated a developing and progressively greater psychological disorganization and inability to meet responsibilities and everyday duties. The family may, indeed, be aware of the problem, wish to implement treatment, but be afraid or wish to avoid the emergency room detention or police arrest. It sould seem appropriate that a special route to the mental health tribunal be available to such families or guardians. The family should be assisted in filling out a comprehensive list of current problems with a statement from the family physician which would accompany the application, medically documenting the facts of the case, particularly the current therapeutic difficulty and reason and need for hospitalization. The letter should not have any conclusionary statements, but should just specify the facts. The mental health tribunal would evaluate such a plea and perhaps *in camera* talk to the family members. If the mental health tribunal, on the basis of these facts, arrived at a decision that psychiatric investigation or treatment was justified, then an order would be issued for the individual to be brought before the mental health tribunal for a psychiatric examination and an attorney would be appointed.

I am aware that this is much more likely to work for the upper or middle classes and for those individuals who have some stability in society than for the indigent. However, one can only hope that with time there will be a greater degree of social stability than is the case at present. But even though this ideal may not be reached for many decades, this route has certain theoretical advantages which should be made available.

A word about the composition of the Mental Health Tribunal:

The Mental Health Tribunal should be composed of a forensically trained psychiatrist, an attorney with *expert* knowledge of human behavior as well as practical experience in dealing with individuals who have psychosocial problems and a representative of the community. Obviously, reasonable supporting staffs should be available to such a tribunal. These may need to consist of a number of consultant psychiatrists, investigative social workers and, of course, secretaries. The mental health tribunal should have as its function the decision-making ability to initiate involuntary treatment as long as certain criteria are met. The tribunal should have within its functional scope the ability to order involuntary inpatient treatment or involuntary (home or convalescent home) ambulatory treatment. Mental health tribunals should have within their scope the ability to recommend the appointment of conservators for patients who are incompetent. The actual implementation, perhaps, should be done in the established legal manner. The tribunal should have a *continued* interest in the patient, and should evaluate the efficacy of treatment and review all hospitalization every month. It should be within the scope of the tribunal to apply certain discretionary judgments initially, but with more stringent criteria as the length of time of treatment progresses. Treatment should be initiated in those cases in which the patient's welfare demands it or in which the interests of his profession, family or property are at stake. It should be limited to only those cases in which the problem is due to a form of mental illness which can be documented as having caused the individual to regress below his optimum level of functioning.

Such a tribunal, if given the option to insist on outpatient care, would probably need to confine very few patients involuntarily, and within a period of time the majority of such patients could be put on outpatient status. The ability to ensure that treatment is continued appropriately would go a long way towards preventing the current state of remissions that clog up the psychiatric institutions. Such a tribunal should have access to sufficient ambulatory care time in the community so that this option is viable, rather than merely theoretical.

One should keep in mind that there are a small number of cases in which the individual, usually as a result of serious organic disease, is in need of custodial care because he is dangerous to himself or unable to take care of himself and in which treatment is likely to be ineffective (e.g. presenile dementias such as Huntington's condition). In such cases confinement would be within the jurisdiction of the tribunal even though therapeutic care is nonexistent.

It is essential to repeat that the psychiatrist should under no circumstance be an advocate for commitment. He should present the findings and his observation, but he should not arrive at conclusionary statement that the patient he has observed is a fit subject for confinement. (7) While he is not necessarily an agent for the patient, since more often than not he is a staff member of an emergency room to which the patient has been brought under some form of coercion, neither is he an agent for any social agency or any particular social viewpoint. His findings should be as unbiased and neutral as possible. If there is anyone who will fill the role of an advocate for commitment of a citizen before such a tribunal, it should be a social agency or a family member.

It would seem reasonable that within the context of presenting data to the tribunal, videotapes of interviews should be used. They could be stored under certain safeguards for a period of time and actually used by the tribunal to refresh their memory as well as to evaluate progress or lack of it. I myself have noticed and most of my colleagues have confirmed the fact that visual memory is very vital, and photographs remind one of students, places, etc. better than written descriptions. Protection for patients could be built into the system by using tapes which self-destruct after a period of time or which would be destroyed by the tribunal.

Most of my recommendations demand a great commitment of professional time as well as significant financial expenditure. At a time when there is a strong revolt of the taxpayer against greater social expenditures and against increased taxation, this may, indeed, be difficult to implement. However, as much as possible, these measures should be within the regular medical budget. And there is every reason to argue that these expenditures should be covered by health insurance.

General Recommendations

In addition to the procedures for such emergency and involuntary hospitalization, there are certain general issues which need to be advocated. As much as possible, there should be a discontinuation of the rural-based psychiatric facilities that have grown up in the United States. Each community up to a certain size should have one and only one emergency psychiatric receiving center. In one community that I know well (a metropolitan population of under half a million), there are six hospitals with six emergency rooms. Most general hospitals can, if they wish, implement treatment of the mentally disturbed, even those sick patients who require seclusion and physical as well as chemical restraints. (8) There is every reason to argue and to develop the concept of the physician's associates. These would be well-trained nurses who work closely under physicians and carry delegated responsibility. A certain amount of screening with some reasonable supervision should entitle such physician's associates to autonomously perform a great amount of psychiatric treatment which is now being done by physicians. In fact, a combination team consisting of a psychiatrist, a couple of physician's associates (that is, trained psychiatric nurses), a pharmacist and a social worker could probably handle a caseload of over 100 ambulatory patients in a very satisfactory and therapeutic manner. It used to be said that what this country needed was a good five-cent cigar. It has now been well said that what this country needs is a good five-dollar-an-hour psychotherapist. Actually, I would think that what the mental health system needs is well-trained psychiatric nurses working as physician's associates in a psychiatric team, who would have limited licenses to prescribed psychotropic medication. (9)

In my own setting, I have successfully taught nurses to do mental status examinations, work as liaison personnel in the emergency room and in medical clinics and to know the indications and adverse effects of most psychotropic medications. In fact, the quality of treatment is enhanced because they more readily assume responsibility for things that they *do* know how to do and ask for help when they get into difficulties, while many psychiatrists in practice or residents in training initially are too hesitant to treat within their competence and then become overconfident and do not ask for advice, when all the indications are that such help is required.

The staffing pattern of psychiatric state facilities could also be markedly changed by developing a new class of specialists. Currently, one of our problems in the United States has been that too many facilities develop residencies only to get young physicians to do the scutwork. The worse the institution, the poorer the quality of the training, the more it approximates a poor apprenticeship rather than a specialist's education. The poorer the quality of the potential student who is attracted by high pay and few education options, the greater the degree of frustration and dissatisfaction with the institution upon finishing. In psychiatry in particular, such physicians who have put in three years as residents and are ostensibly trained to practice the specialty of psychiatry open up private offices and abandon the state hospital as soon as they are licensed to do so! The state hospital has thus lost a physician who was at least able to function in the setting of the hospital and who had certain expertise in inpatient treatment, while the community gets someone who is usually quite incompetent in the practice of office psychiatry.(10)

There should be training programs which would attract physicians to the state facilities. The training programs could be kept to a minimum — six to twelve months — and the physician, after that period of time, would be accepted as a mental health physician. Together such physicians and psychiatric nurses could manage an inpatient work load.

Very few statutes make any specific provision for discharge. It appears that the concern of most jurisdictions is towards sharpening the indications for involuntary admission and then building into the system a number of workable and reasonable protective overseeing devices. These are annual or semiannual reviews by probate judges, courts and mental health tribunals. Of course, during this time the patient also has the option for a habeas corpus proceeding. Yet often the habeas corpus proceedings have been criticized as looking into the legality of the commitment action rather than, necessarily, the indications for its initiation.

It is interesting here, that the Polish statutes regarding the treatment of the mentally ill do address themselves very seriously to the problem of discharge, giving the physician broad powers to discharge when the patient is well and to conditionally discharge to a convalescent home, or conditionally discharge at the request of a family member or a friend who undertakes to take care of the patient. (11) I do not know how well this works in practice, but it brings up some interesting and opportune ideas.

Many have argued that psychiatric services belong in the area of human resources. Undoubtedly, large numbers of physically as well as mentally ill people do need prolonged convalescent care. Many mentally ill people need someone to manage their affairs. There are facilities needed for those who are physically and also psychosocially unable to function in our currently highly technological world. As a psychiatric consultant for the social security administration law judges, I am invariably asked to review claimants' psychiatric histories. On the basis of the reports which are obtained by the claimant, I am supposed to advise the judge whether medical criteria of permanent disability are met. I am then asked to undertake an assessment of how they are met! Most of these cases are difficult, since the easy ones with clear-cut disability will most likely have had their claims honored in previous adjudications. Yet the majority of the claimants who come to the appeal process and who advance this particular psychiatric claim do not have clearcut medical or psychiatric evidence to substantiate their claim of permanent disability. many, indeed, claim psychiatric disability but have consistently avoided, sabotaged or failed to meaningfully cooperate in any kind of psychiatric treatment that has been suggested or prescribed. They are obviously more interested in substantiating the permanence of their illness than in attempting to become self-sufficient.

The problem is indeed one of motivation. Motivation, as we know it, is something that has developed in childhood and becomes part of the attributes of the personality — for most of us, a positive attribute of a "sound" character. Those who, in the process of their lives, have failed to develop such internal motivations merely become the passive victims of social coercion or of reward. In the past, society dealt with such people by coercion and by threats. Currently, that is unacceptable; yet we have few rewards. The best we can do is to suggest an internal pride at surmounting adversity. Unfortunately, for most the only reward is a guaranteed income.

Our society has, at this historical time and in this cultural context, accepted that people who need care will be cared for and not neglected. Yet we are far behind eastern Europe in providing reasonable sheltered homes for those who need some sufficient and graduated freedom and social interaction so as to prevent further social regression.

In the United States the exercise of freedom has too often led to what can only be described as a destructive freedom. People are put in welfare hotels in the middle of high crime districts so that they are afraid to go out; they are given their money, and at the same time the boredom and lack of opportunity for any kind of socially approved behavior channels these people into chronic alcoholism. (12) Sheltered workshops are necessary, and some individuals can be successfully and fully rehabilitated by such processes, though the majority settle at that level of competence. The sheltered workshop can give a certain feeling of personal satisfaction and even some monetary reward. Careful attention, obviously, has to be given to prevent the kind of abuses of indentured labor that occurred in some state psychiatric facilities, but even here the abuses have been overexaggerated. The critics of this system have argued that work in a state facility can only be termed therapeutic if the same would be the case in a private hospital. That, I think, is an appealing idea, but closer analysis reveals certain flaws. An attorney, hospitalized for his depression, may very well enjoy paddle tennis, bridge, or the theater. During the evening he may get a great degree of satisfaction from catching up on his reading or studying the stock market. Patients from the lower socioeconomic groups are often not interested in any such pursuits and relate best in working situations.

There are many individuals who, because of their alcoholism, because of drug addiction or because of advanced age are only partially able to manage their financial affairs. The New Zealand statutes speak of these people as the mentally impaired as opposed to the mentally ill. Conservatorship for this group to handle their income and property should be the rule.

This, therefore, becomes my final suggestion for the mental health tribunal and its function — the power to order such a convalescent setting on the recommendation of the hospital staff if there is no family or family objection. Understandably, the individual should have a right to oppose or at any time appeal against such a process, but the benign neglect of the chronically mentally ill that we see in the name of freedom is a moral disgrace and a social cruelty. This would be the last link in a comprehensive development of services that would span the medical aspect and the human resource aspect of the treatment, care and rehabilitation of the mentally disabled, the mentally ill as well as the mentally impaired.

Furthermore, emergency detention and involuntary hospitalization should be protected by very strict and meaningful laws and statutes pertaining to confidentiality and privileged communication which would in no way impede the professions' sharing the knowledge for the welfare of the patient.

The actions of the tribunal would be subject to review by a higher court.

SUMMARY OF SUGGESTIONS

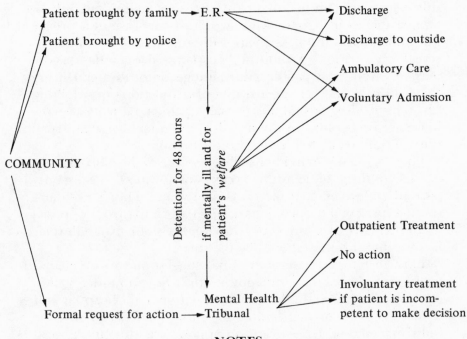

NOTES

1. For example, the difference between a developed country like the United States and a developing, emerging country like India is a good example of what I have in mind. The problem in India is still one of basic epidemiological illness, the eradication of smallpox and the eradication of nutritional disorders. Physical health and preventive care, particularly of the youngsters, may very well be a greater social and moral priority than the sensitivity to individual rights and protection of civil liberties of the mentally ill.

2. A draft Act governing hospitalization of the mentally ill was prepared by a group of the National Institute of Mental Health and the Office of General Counsel of the United States. It was issued as Public Health Service Publication No. 51 and printed by the United States Government Printing Office in 1952. It is reprinted in full as Appendix A in S. J. Brackel, and R. S. Rock, *The Mentally Disabled and the Law* (Chicago, University of Chicago Press, 1971).

3. W. Overholser, and H. Wiehoen, "Commitment of the Mentally Ill," *American Journal of Psychiatry*, 102:758-769 (1946). They conclude their review of the problems pertaining to the commitment of the mentally ill by quoting Isaac Ray from the paper "Confinement of the Insane." For the actual writings of Isaac Ray, the reader is referred to *Contributions to Mental Pathology* (Boston, Little, Brown & Co., 1873). This is a collection of Isaac Ray's works and includes his famous paper "Confinement of the Insane," originally published by the *American Law Review* in 1869. This book was reprinted in 1973 as a facsimile by Scholars, Facsimiles and Reprints, Delmar, New York.

4. For a good review of the English and Welsh system of implementing the functioning of the involuntary commitment and review see J. C. Wood, "Mental health Review Tribunals," *Medical Science and Law*, 7:86-92 (1971). The New York State laws pertaining to hospitalization are Article 31 of the New York State Mental Hygiene Law. For a description of the function, see R. K. Gupta, "New York's Mental Health Information Service: An experiment in Due Process," *Rutgers Law Review*, 25:405-450 (1971).

5. Webster defines a profession as, "a calling requiring specialized knowledge and after long and intensive preparation including instructions in skills and methods as well as in the scientific, historical or scholarly principles underlying such skills and methods, maintaining by force of organization or concerted opinion high standards of achievement and conduct and committing its members to continued study and to a kind of work which has for its prime purpose, the rendering of a public service."

6. Two recent articles have documented the difficulty of predicting dangerousness in individual cases and the fact that psychiatrists have little expertise in such actuarial data. B. Rubin, "Prediction of Dangerousness in law and psychiatry," *Journal of Psychiatry and Law*, 1:409-426 (1973).

7. I am particularly familiar with the State of Connecticut and its operations. The probate judge who makes a ruling on an equity basis as to the need for prolonged involuntary hospitalization of a patient does so on the advice of two physicians, one of whom has to be a psychiatrist and neither of whom can be employees of the hospital or related to the individual. These experts advise the judge in terms of the following: that, after having examined the patient they have found such person as "mentally ill and a fit subject for confinement in a

hospital for mental illness." Such conclusionary and archaic language is exactly the issue which has caused considerable and understandable concern within the legal profession.

8. G. R. Reding, and B. Maguire, "Non-segregated acute psychiatric admissions to general hospitals — continuity of care within the community hospital," *New England Journal of Medicine,* 289:185-189 (1973).

9. A. DiMascio, "It's about Time," *International Journal of Psychiatry,* 10:87-89 (1972). In this paper, Dr. DiMascio advances and advocates a very reasonable plan to have psychiatric nurses empowered to prescribe limited forms of medications.

10. One of the problems in state facilities is the heavy use of foreign medical graduates whose general knowledge of English, the social context and cultural background is, at times, limited. Often such physicians have no inherent interest in psychiatry, but do so because this is the only place where they can find employment without obtaining or qualifying for a license. For a comprehensive discussion of this, see Footnote #16, Chapter II.

11. The regulations pertaining to commitment are an executive order emanating from the Minister of Health (Minister Zdrowia) and promulgated on the 15th of December, 1952 in the official Ministry News as order #120/52. I have been unable to document that this is anything but an internal medical decision and am not aware of any legislative action behind this order. I was given to understand by a number of people that the legal profession in Poland is not happy with these regulations and would like to see them modified.

12. "The discharged chronic mental patient," *Medical World News,* 15:47-58 (1974). Also, the legal problem of a city barring mental patients: "City restrained from barring Mental Patients," *Psychiatric News,* (July 3rd, 1974).

CHAPTER VIII

CONCLUSIONS

It is probably a truism, but nonetheless quite pertinent, that the current acrimony in the area of the involuntary hospitalization for certain groups of the mentally ill has developed into a "right" versus "wrong" debate. Both sides, on one hand the rank and file of the psychiatric profession and on the other hand many of the very dedicated and concerned attorneys, see themselves as wearing the white hats of inherent integrity and see their opposition as oppressive, benighted and reactionary. As a concern, the issue has sparked more life in the legal profession than it has in the medical, or, specifically, in the psychiatric group. Attorneys have developed courses in commitment laws and have generally become very interested in and dedicated to protecting the "rights" of the mentally ill. (1) That these rights need to be protected and that, in fact, many of the mentally ill patients have been tremendously abused by society (this abuse being hallmarked by neglect and lack of treatment) is indeed a fact. What the medical profession has reacted to is a certain naivete and arrogance among many of the attorneys who have enthusiastically condemned, confronted, criticized and challenged the practices of organized psychiatry, but actually have failed to come up with any practical or constructive alternatives. (2) To deny the existence of mental illness and to praise voluntary admission is hardly a constructive or thoughtful suggestion.

However, the interest and the concern is there and, undoubtedly, should be fostered so that the greatest benefit can be obtained from this current wave of concern.

This monograph has attempted to synthesize an historical and cross-cultural perspective of the problem of involuntary hospitalization.

Being a physician and a psychiatrist, I undoubtedly have shown medical bias in presenting and discussing the material. I would hope that it has not been a completely uncritical presentation, but rather one that attempts to show the problems currently faced by our society and the tragedy and plight of that group of helpless people, however labeled, who have not been able to make it in society.

It is also undoubtedly true and can be documented that the profession of law has, in the last twenty-five years, shown far more effort at coming to an understanding of the behavioral sciences in general and of psychiatry in particular than the profession of medicine has shown in understanding sociology or legal philosophy. A number of studies have documented that the American law schools have attempted to teach psychiatry and psychological knowledge to their professional students. (3) A review of legal periodicals shows a consistent and uniformly excellent effort at presenting psychological and psychiatric knowledge and in integrating these findings with the practice of the legal profession. This has been done more consistently and over a longer period of time than anything that has been attempted in the medical schools as far as jurisprudence is concerned.

Many of the approaches to the teaching of law students have been extensively described, and while some authors have emphasized the teaching of the philosophy of the psychiatric profession, others have emphasized the clinical experience. (4)

Authors have described the difficulties and the various techniques. Unfortunately, one of the threads which runs through many of the papers and, indeed, through some of the books is a recognition of the inherent hostility between the two professions. Titles such as "Cold war or Entente Cordiale" or "The pursuit of agreement" keep coming through and illustrating the basic division. (5)

To the medical man, the attorney comes across as an individual who will embark as an advocate for his client regardless of the moral right or wrong. (6) He will combat the case using all the tricks of the adversary proceeding to buttress his case, discredit the adversary and, in the process, obtain his contingency fee. The average physician perceives the average attorney not so much as a posessor of a certain philosophical and professional discipline, but as a man who will distort the truth, argue from the particular to the general, use glib language and sue the innocent physician for malpractice and deprive a sick patient of treatment merely to obtain his release.

The attorney, on the other hand, sees the physician as a member of a guild that refuses to be accountable to society, who hides behind technical language, who practices his profession in a high-handed way and who is unable or unwilling to explain what he does in a court of law. Furthermore, in the commitment process, he sees the physician — and specifically the psychiatrist — as usurping to himself those inherent rights which the constitution guarantees exclusively to the legal process. He sees that physician as being unwilling to become more open, as claiming all kinds of privileged status and as defending his monopoly at the expense of society. (7) Therefore, he readily accepts those critics emanating from the psychiatric profession as Szasz who have castigated the profession for their lack of clarity; he assaults the grandiosity of psychiatry and finds support among those who have criticized psychiatry for having abandoned a role which was historically that of healer and for having become in some ways the guardians of the establishment. (8)

The psychiatrist perceives in the attorney an individual who writes books such as *Prisoners of Psychiatry,* in which a number of cases are described that have all been given the benefit of criminal and adversary proceedings and are being held by the criminal process. At best, he sees in such a presentation of facts a gross ignorance or even a conscious malevolence and dishonesty alien to worthy scholarship. (9)

The educational process is a very complicated one, but it appears to at least consist of two very important aspects: a cognitive as well as an attitudinal development. The cognitive has to do with information and knowledge, whether it be philosophical, theoretical or factual. The attitudinal has to do much more with more subtle, harder to measure emotional experiences which affect and modify the perception of problems. Most of our educational system is elaborately structured in developing the cognitive aspects and only unconsciously or intuitively in developing the attitudinal ones. In a medical school, attitudinal changes can be particularly well documented at a time when the student begins to have direct patient contact and some minimal medical responsibility. Once professionalization develops, it begins to affect the student's perception of his role, his own self-image and his function. This process, in the medical school, is one of the most interesting, one of the most exciting and yet at the same time inherently troublesome. While we are all glad when our young students begin to develop patterns of behavior that we prize highly such as responsibility, punctuality, high level of expertise and concern, at the same time there is a feeling of concern that young people who are so articulate in their autonomy and their own particular expressions of life style will begin to conform to the demands of their older colleagues.

The same, apparently, seems to hold true for the law student. He very quickly develops the attitudes of the academic law professor. These are highly libertarian, extremely intellectual and have comparatively little base in the realities of everyday legal practice. The interest in law and psychiatry is not so much to learn the strength and attributes of the legal profession or to study human problems, but it is to learn how to pick holes and to show the psychiatrist up in court. (10) This is comparable to the interests of the average physicians in law, which are not how to uphold the legal rights of the patient or to make sure that the spirit of the law is obeyed or to understand juridical ethics, but merely to stay out of malpractice trouble and to practice "defensive" medicine.

To teach the problems, it is important to try and involve the student in participating in the decision-making process. A merely cognitive and intellectual approach may be the only way that the faculty of the law school will accept such a course. It may, indeed, be the only way that students may be attracted to participate in such a course. Yet the most crucial and the most educational aspect of educating both the attorney and the psychiatrist is to have them work together on the common problem. (11)

I have advocated and have tried to implement as much as is possible just such an approach. There are major problems of scheduling and, at times, what appear to be insurmountable problems of professional concern. Law students are unhappy at participating in the observation of medical cases when problems of informed consent and possible conflict of interest have not been settled to their complete satisfaction. Yet once these difficulties can be surmounted and such students placed in a relationship of working with the medical student or the psychiatric resident, then very great benefits of mutual development can be observed. It is in this area of attitudinal change through a practical approach that the greatest benefit and the most significant teaching of these serious problems can be accomplished.

There is no easy way of doing this and, unfortunately, law schools are as pressed for time in their curriculum as are medical schools. This is unfortunate and potentially quite tragic. Medicine has at least recognized that the basic medical school curriculum is, at best, a modicum of preparation and that another three years, at least, of specialist's training is imperative. At this point, the number of physicians going into general practice is quite small. The legal profession, in this respect, is still a century behind and has a long way to go; and while one would not expect an attorney who has no interest in psychological problems as such and whose intention is to open up a private practice of law dealing primarily with tax matters and search titles to understand psychological theory, it *is* rather unfortunate that many attorneys who *are* interested in these complex problems (in which their expertise can only help rather than harm) are deprived of specialty training following their graduation. They then have recourse to two-day courses in the Practicing Law Institute which, in two days and in three volumes, teaches the interested attorney all that he allegedly and confidently needs to know about psychiatric practice, psychiatric history, nosology and treatment so that he is, as it were, trained to pursue the legal rights of the mentally handicapped.

In clinical medicine it has been well said that to limit teaching to clinical work is akin to sailing without navigating instruments. To just study books and not to treat patients is like staying ashore and learning navigation. The same holds true for law students. To give them theoretical material without practical exposure is merely to teach them navigating without feeling or seeing the sea around them. To throw them on the open sea without giving them a feeling for the intellectual part of the problem is to deprive them of navigational aids.

A couple of books have, indeed, been written specifically in this area, and they have much to offer. However, whether the books used are specifically those written for law students or whether they are selections of papers made up by the instructor is immaterial. (12) It is important that the teaching be done in an interdisciplinary fashion and that the course itself be perceived as an ongoing laboratory experience in which issues are confronted and feelings are expressed and discussed. It is important, as much as possible and as much as scheduling permits, that there be a mixture of medical and law students, so that there is no single majority of any one discipline.

While the subject of this monograph has been primarily the issue of involuntary hospitalization, the problem that has to be taught is greater in perspective than just this issue. The problems have to do with motivation with understanding the problems of informed consent, of disposition, of testamentary capacity and generally of criminal accountability. But there is no better way for teaching an attorney the problems of human distress than for him to find himself in the emergency room observing a distressed patient, and there is *nothing* which changes a psychiatrist's attitude towards his inherent conviction that what he does is best for the patient than to be forced to justify his actions to an eager and critical law student participating in the interview.

NOTES

1. B. J. Ennis, and P. R. Friedman, *Legal Rights of the Mentally Handicapped* (New York, Practicing Law Institute, The Mental Health Law Project, 1973).

2. Most of the legal activity in the area of mental health has been to either work towards prohibitive commitment legislation which would restrict commitments to problems of dangerousness, as in Washington, D.C. where the criteria are that (Article 21-521): "Any accredited officer, agent or physician who has reason to believe that a person is mentally ill and because of his illness is likely to injure himself or others if he's not immediately detained may, without a warrant, take the person into custody, transport him to a public or private hospital, make application for his admission thereto for purposes of emergency observation and

diagnosis." Even the author of the most recently successful right to treatment lawsuit, Dr. M. Birnbaum, who has written extensively in this area, "The Right to Treatment — Some comments on Implementation," *Duquesne Law Review,* 10:579-608 (1972), and who, for his efforts on behalf of the incarcerated patients was awarded the Manfred Guttmacher prize for forensic psychiatry in 1973, admitted that his perception of much of the activity of the legal profession and their involvement in this area was one of wishing to abolish all state hospitals. These remarks were made at the Taylor Manor Hospital Psychiatric Symposium in April, 1974 and will appear in print published by Williams and Wilkins in the fall of 1974.

3. The legal literature is quite prolific in the area of psychiatry. The various law reviews of the prominent law schools have considerable numbers of excellent articles on the problems of law and psychiatry or on the problems of teaching psychiatry and the behavioral sciences to law students. This can, under no circumstance, be considered a comprehensive list, but is an example of the kind of writing. H. Wechsler, "The Criteria of Criminal Responsibility," *University of Chicago Law Review,* 22:367-396 (1954-1955); R. Slovenko, "Civil Commitment in Perspective," *Journal of Public Law,* 20:3-32 (1971); L. Silverstein, "Psychology, Mental Illness and the Law," *West Virginia Law Review,* 60:55-70 and 133-165 (1957-1958); D. F. Ryer, "Comment: The Mentally Ill in Connecticut," *Connecticut Law Review,* 6:303-359 (1973-1974); J. Robitscher, "The Right to Psychiatric Treatment: A Social Approach to the Plight of the State Hospital Patient," *Villanove Law Review,* 18:11-36 (1972); R. E. Potts, "The Psychological Implications of the Practice of Divorce Law," *Ohio State Law Journal,* 14:168-182 (1953); Y. Kumasaka, and R. K. Gupta, "Lawyers and Psychiatrists in the Court: Issues in Civil Commitment," *Maryland Law Review,* 32:3-41 (1972); W. G. Katz, "Law, Psychiatry and Free Will," *University of Chicago Law Review,* 22:397-404 (1954-1955). Case Comment: "Wyatt vs. Stickney and the Right of Civilly Committed Mental Patients to adequate treatment," *Harvard Law Review,* 86:1282-1305 (1973); J. Goldstein, and J. Katz, "Abolish the Insanity Defense, Why Not?," *Yale Law Journal,* 72:853-876 (1963); J. N. Frank, "Judicial Fact finding and Psychology," *Ohio State Law Journal,* 14:183-189 (1953). This selection just gives the flavor of the continuous provocative and scholarly work that is published in the legal literature.

4. Some of the more prominent authors describing various styles of teaching have been well summarized by Professor Ralph Slovenko in his *Psychiatry and Law,* (Boston, Little, Brown, 1973) in the appendix Selected Readings — General, pages 613-616.

5. S. Glueck, *Law and Psychiatry: Cold War or Entente Cordiale?* (Baltimore, Johns Hopkins Paperbacks, 1966), and J. B. Robitscher, *Pursuit of Agreement — Psychiatry and the Law* (Philadelphia, J. B. Lippincott, 1966).

6. M. Hancock, "Conflict, Drama and Magic in the early English law," *Ohio State Law Journal*, 14:119-137 (1953) describes the evolution of the attorney as an advocate and champion of the litigant. This is a fascinating article describing the early forms of trial by water and by grasping a hot piece of iron and the adjudication of guilt or innocence on the basis of those results. Furthermore, it describes the primitive form of jury, the development of the champion, then the progressively greater ritualization of laws of evidence. Seen in that perspective, the attorney is indeed a paid advocate (or champion) to do everything possible to tilt on behalf of his client, even to keep truth hidden and cause anguish and suffering to some innocent members of society. The recent case from New York State in which attorneys knew about a murder but did not inform the authorities and kept the parents of the murdered child in suspense is accepted and condoned by canon ethics, but revolting to the moral and common sense attitude of most citizens!

7. D. L. Bazelon, "Psychiatrists and the Adversary Process," *Scientific American*, 230:18-23 (1974).

8. T. S. Szasz, *Law, Liberty and Psychiatry* (New York, MacMillan, 1963), and the most recently published book by E. F. Torrey, *The Death of Psychiatry* (Radner, Tilton Book Company, 1974). This book was advertised in the American Psychiatric Association News, July 3, 1974 as "Doctor Torrey administers the coup de grace to an overage and hurtful discipline. For everyone who thinks psychiatrists are Gods and everyone who thinks psychiatrists are frauds." The cover of the book describes it as "an eminent psychiatrist uses his well-functioning crap detector to administer the coup de grace to an overage and hurtful discipline."

9. B. Ennis, *Prisoners of Psychiatry: Mental Patients, Psychiatrists and the Law* (New York, Harcourt, Brace & Jovanovich, 1972). The author of this book describes a number of cases of criminals, tried and incarcerated in maximum security hospitals, all of them having been given the benefit of an adversary proceeding so warmly advocated by Judge Bazelon. See supra note #7.

10. See supra note #1. The following is a verbatim piece of advice to an attorney acting on behalf of an incarcerated patient:

> If there is a hearing before a neutral psychiatric arbiter, concentrate all of your effort into getting him or her incensed with the inadequacy of the hospital psychiatrist, the facility and the treatment resources. This may not be hard to do in many cases; the hospital psychiatrist is likely to be foreign, poorly trained, under-staffed and over-worked. The board psychiatrist will probably be much more 'establishment' and orthodox. Put him in the position of either having to endorse what the hospital wants to do — of having to underwrite obvious inadequacy or

of being willing to go after the inadequacies himself on behalf of the patient.

11. M. Peszke, "What kind of psychiatry in Law School?," *Journal of Legal Education*, 23:309-317 (1971), and R. Slovenko, *Law and Psychiatry*, supra note #4. Also, J. Zusman, and W. A. Carnahan, "Psychiatry and the Law: Changing the System through changing the training," *American Journal of Psychiatry*, 131:915-918 (1974).

12. For the physician, the best book in the area of psychiatry and law is, undoubtedly, R. Slovenko, *Psychiatry and Law*, supra note 4. Professor Slovenko (an attorney and a psychologist) was awarded the Manfred Guttmacher prize for 1974 for his excellent work in the area of forensic psychiatry. For the student in the law class who is trying to obtain a comprehensive idea of the various problems in the area of psychiatry the following is recommended: R. C. Allen, A. Zenoff, and J. G. Rubin,: *Readings in Law and Psychiatry* (Baltimore, Johns Hopkins Press, 1968). It is my understanding that a new edition of this book is being published. Also see Chapter IX and suggested readings.

FURTHER READINGS AND
GENERAL COMMENTS

IT is my hope that the reader of this book, whether he be a physician, lawyer or an interested layman, will be prompted to read further. The literature of both professions is so divergent in nature that attorneys are confused by medical periodicals, and physicians, even more so by legal journals.

In medicine, the pattern is for each of the specialties and subspecialties to have its own periodicals — usually monthly, occasionally quarterly. Within a specialty such as psychiatry there may be different journals emphasizing psycho-pharmacology, psychosomatics, psychoanalysis, community psychiatry, etc. It is a tricky issue to mention any of the periodicals by name and omit others, since that may be unwittingly taken as a sign of criticism of the ones omitted. But in view of the fact that the English language has probably over a hundred strictly psychiatric journals, not to mention clinical psychology periodicals, it is impossible to mention all of them. Any medical center library, however, will provide a listing of all psychiatric periodicals that are published.

For the instructor or student of legal psychiatry the following, however, should be noted and ordered: *Bulletin of American Academy of Psychiatry and the Law,* which is a quarterly and published by the American Academy of Psychiatry and the Law, and the *Journal of Psychiatry and Law.* The Academy of Psychiatry and Law (AAPL) also holds two scientific meetings a year devoted strictly to the topics of legal psychiatry. There is also an American Academy of Forensic Sciences which has a psychiatric section and publishes a quarterly — *Journal of Forensic Sciences.*

In addition to those periodicals, the United States has a number of psychiatric monthlies, among them being the following:

1. The *American Journal of Psychiatry* is the official periodical of the American Psychiatric Association. it reports many of the original papers that are submitted at the annual scientific meeting sponsored by the Association.

2. *Archives of General Psychiatry* is a most prestigious monthly and is devoted to general problems of psychiatry.

3. *Journal of Psychosomatic Medicine* is devoted to problems relating to the psyche and soma.

4. *Psychiatry,* an outstanding quarterly, is devoted to an interdisciplinary approach to the study of personality and interpersonal problems.

The philosophy of all these periodicals is that they present research data or original viewpoints, and all of them are rather scanty in review articles.

Quite unlike medicine, the legal profession has not emphasized specialty training or, for that matter, even clinical teaching to the same extent. The pattern is particularly different and quite idiosyncratic for law, since the most advanced, provocative and thoughtful articles are written in the Law School Reviews. These are edited and published by students, and eminent guest writers present their viewpoints. The commentaries in the Law Reviews are also outstanding review articles of considerable length and scholarship which medicine would do well to emulate. (1) The Law Review periodicals, however, cover a variety of legal subjects so that one has to check the index to see whether the topic of legal psychiatry has been touched on in any given year. The most outstanding Law Reviews are put out by the top prestigious law schools of the country such as Yale, Harvard, Chicago, Michigan, etc.

There are a number of scientific meetings each year that address themselves to the topic of legal psychiatry, and occasionally the proceedings are published in full or in part. But except for the groups that actually hold annual meetings at definite dates, such as the American Academy of Psychiatry and the Law, the meetings are ad hoc arrangements. Yet, obviously, some of these attract outstanding speakers, and the quality of the presentations and discussions is above average. Recent examples were the Taylor Manor Hospital sponsored symposium on "Medical,

Moral and Legal Issues in Mental Health Care." This will be published as a book in 1974 by Williams and Wilkins. Another excellent symposium was Butler Hospital's Isaac Ray Symposium, "Human Rights, the Law and Psychiatric Treatment," which will be published in a forthcoming *Bulletin of the American Academy of Psychiatry and the Law*. The Isaac Ray award lectures are held every year; the speakers are by invitation, and the proceedings are published as a monograph.

The field of forensic or legal psychiatry suffers from a paucity of texts. The interests of the professions are so divergent, but even more so is the different approach to education in both professional schools. Medicine is, by and large, oriented towards clinical material and the perusal of new research. Unfortunately, most of the forensic psychiatry works have been written with a very narrow view — namely to help the physician in his day-to-day problems of confronting legal issues, such as submitting a psychiatric report to a court, understanding testamentary capacity or insuring adequate malpractice coverage. However, two works are outstanding in this area:

1. Davidson, H.: *Forensic Psychiatry*, 2nd ed. New York, Ronald Press, 1965, and

2. Robitscher, J. B.: *Pursuit of Agreement: Psychiatry and the Law*. Philadelphia, J. B. Lippincott, 1966.

Law school teaching and academic interest is predominantly oriented to perusal of significant literature and review of problems. Hence, the nature of the texts used primarily by attorneys is significantly different and, therefore, in this area the books that have attracted the greatest degree of interest have been materials such as:

Katz, J., Goldstein, J., and Dershowitz, A. M.: *Psychoanalysis, Psychiatry and Law*, New York, Free Press, 1967.

Allen, R. C., Ferster, E. Z., and Rubin, J. G.: *Readings in Law and Psychiatry*. Baltimore, Johns Hopkins University Press, 1968.

The material is presented in the traditional legal manner. It is raw data from law decisions, psychiatric texts, sociology, etc., and it is left for class discussion. Inevitably, the class discussion and the comments are determined by the instructor's understanding of the material, his own idiosyncracy with which he approaches the problem, as well as the slant that he wants to emphasize. Both books have great popularity among law school professors, since they reflect their established patterns of teaching, but the physician (or, for that matter, the layman) will find them quite unhelpful in confronting the issues of ethics, informed consent, right to treatment or of understanding autonomy.

However 1973 saw a significant breakthrough in the publication of Professor Ralph Slovenko's *Law and Psychiatry,* Boston, Little, Brown, 1973. This book significantly adds to the material available, and it is the first book which presents general legal philosophy pertaining to medical and to psychiatric problems in particular in a manner understandable to the reader. This book answers the need of the interested and concerned physician as well as providing a good insight into legal thinking.

Outside of this, I know of no books on general law which may be applicable to the physician.

However, the attorney should be aware of some good general texts in psychiatry. Too often, as I have written in the body of the monograph, psychoanalysis and psychiatry are treated as synoymous, and Freud's introductory lectures are considered as the end-all of psychiatric theory. Here is a list of some books that should be considered and included in any general reading in a law and psychiatry class:

Hinsie, L. E., and Campbell, R. J.: *Psychiatric Dictionary.* London, Oxford University Press, 1960.

American Psychiatric Association — Committee on Public Information: *A Psychiatric Glossary,* 2nd ed. American Psychiatric Association, 1964.

Waelder, R.: *Basic Theory of Psychoanalysis.* New York, Schocken Books, 1960.

Cameron, N. A.: *Personality Development and Psychopathology, A Dynamic Approach.* Boston, Houghton Mifflin Co., 1963.

Hartmann, H., Kris, E., and Loewenstein, R. M.: *Papers on Psychoanalytic Psychology.* New York, International Universities Press, 1964.

Sigerist, H. E.: *A History of Medicine,* London, Oxford

University Press, 1951-1961.

Pincus, J., and Tucker, G.: *Behavioral Neurology*. London, Oxford University Press, 1974.

Mark, V. H., and Ervin, F. R.: *Violence and the Brain*. Hagerstown, Harper & Row, 1970.

Lidz, T.: *The Origin and Treatment of Schizophrenic Disorders*. New York, Basic Books, 1973.

Galdston, I. (Ed.): *The Interface between Psychiatry and Anthropology*. New York, Brunner/Mazel, 1971.

Davis, D. R.: *An Introduction to Psychopathology*, 3rd ed., London, Oxford University Press, 1973.

Cooper, J. R., Bloom, F. E., and Roth, R. H.: *The Biochemical Basis of Neuropharmacology*. London, Oxford University Press, 1970.

Rosenthal, D., and Kety, S. S. (Ed.).: *The Transmission of Schizophrenia*. London, Pergamon Press, 1968.

Lidz, T., Fleck, S., and Cornelison, A. R.: *Schizophrenia and the Family*. New York, International Universities Press, 1966.

Marmor, J.: *Modern Psychoanalysis; New Directions and Perspectives*. New York, Basic Books, 1968.

Kiev, A.: *Magic, Faith, and Healing; Studies in Primitive Psychiatry Today*. Riverside, Free Press of Glencoe, 1964.

Wolberg, L. R.: *The Technique of Psychotherapy*. New York, Grune & Stratton, 1967.

Jaspers, K.: *General Psychopathology*. Chicago, University of Chicago Press, 1963.

Redlich, F. C., and Freedman, D. X.: *The Theory and Practice of Psychiatry*. New York, Basic Books, 1966.

Alexander, F. G., and Ross, H. (Eds.): *Dynamic Psychiatry*. Chicago, University of Chicago Press, 1952.

Galdston, I. (Ed.): *Historic Derivations of Modern Psychiatry*. New York, McGraw-Hill, 1967.

White, R. W.: *The Abnormal Personality*. New York, Ronald Press, 1964.

NOTE

1. See footnote #3, Chapter VIII.

AUTHOR INDEX

147

SUBJECT INDEX